Selected Poems and Letters of

Emily Dickinson

TOGETHER WITH

Thomas Wentworth Higginson's

ACCOUNT OF HIS CORRESPONDENCE

WITH THE POET AND HIS VISIT

TO HER IN *Amherst*

EDITED, WITH AN INTRODUCTION,
BY *Robert N. Linscott*

This is my letter to the world,
That never wrote to me...

W9-BLE-096

ANCHOR BOOKS

DOUBLEDAY

New York London Toronto Sydney Auckland

AN ANCHOR BOOK
PUBLISHED BY DOUBLEDAY
a division of Bantam Doubleday Dell Publishing Group, Inc.
1540 Broadway, New York, New York 10036

ANCHOR BOOKS, DOUBLEDAY, and the portrayal of an anchor
are trademarks of Doubleday, a division of Bantam Doubleday
Dell Publishing Group, Inc.

The Anchor Books edition is the first publication
of *Selected Poems and Letters of Emily Dickinson*,
edited by Robert N. Linscott.

ISBN 0-385-09423-X

Library of Congress Catalog Card Number 59-12052
Copyright © 1959 by Robert N. Linscott

Introduction

Emily Dickinson was born on December 10, 1830, in a New England where Puritanism was dying and literature was just coming to life. Her birthplace was Amherst, a quiet village in the Connecticut Valley of Massachusetts, nearly a hundred miles from Concord and Cambridge in space, and at least half that number of years in time. Here she lived a life, outwardly uneventful, inwardly dedicated to a secret and self-imposed assignment—the mission of writing a "letter to the world" that would express, in poems of absolute truth and of the utmost economy, her concepts of life and death, of love and nature, and of what Henry James called "the landscape of the soul."

Unpublished in her lifetime, unknown at her death in 1886, her poems, by chance and good fortune, reached, at last, the world to which they had been addressed. "If fame belonged to me," she had written in 1862, "I could not escape her; if she did not, the longest day would pass me on the chase, and the approbation of my dog would forsake me." The long day passed and fame was finally hers; fame not only for her poetry, but for her personal history.

From her family Emily had love without understanding. Her father, leading lawyer of the village, and, in later life, treasurer of Amherst College and member of the legislature and of Congress, dominated the household. "His heart was pure and terrible," Emily wrote after his death in 1874, "and I think no other like it exists." Her gentle, colorless mother lived in his shadow. Austin, the only son, patterned himself on his father but lacked the formidable self-righteousness of the old Puritan. Lavinia, crotchety and outspoken, was watchdog and protector of her shy, sensitive, and sometimes rebellious sister. The family lived in a brick mansion set in spacious grounds on Amherst's main street, and neither sister ever married.

After two years at Amherst Academy and one at the Mount Holyoke Female Seminary, Emily Dickinson settled down to the customary life of a New England village. Many years later a school friend remembered her as "not beautiful, yet she had great beauties. Her eyes were lovely auburn, soft and warm, her hair lay in rings of the same color all over her head, and her skin and teeth were fine. She had a demure manner which brightened easily into fun where she felt at home, but among strangers she was rather shy, silent, and even deprecating. She was exquisitely neat and careful in her dress, and always had flowers about her. She was one of the wits of the school, and there were no signs in her life and character of the future recluse."

Into her life during these years came two young men who may have had some slight influence on her career: Leonard Humphrey, principal of Amherst Academy, and Benjamin F. Newton, a law student in her father's office. Both stimulated her interest in books; Newton encouraged her to write. Both died young and were remembered in the lines:

I never lost as much but twice,
And that was in the sod;
Twice I have stood a beggar
Before the door of God!

Reticence was a Dickinson characteristic, and most of what we know or surmise about Emily's emotional life comes by inference from her poems and letters. Sometime during her twenties she had begun seriously to write poetry; just when cannot be known because her early poems were destroyed, or are unidentifiable as such. By 1858 she was copying her poems in ink and gathering them together in little packets, loosely bound by thread. In that year she appears to have written fifty-two poems. In 1862 there was an astonishing total of three hundred and fifty-six. In 1865 the number had fallen off to eighty-five, and thereafter averaged about twenty a year.

The fuse that touched off the creative explosion of the early sixties appears to have been a Philadelphia clergyman: Charles Wadsworth, forty-one years old, a husband and a father when Emily Dickinson met him in May, 1855, while on her way home from a visit to her father in Washington. Correspondence must have followed since drafts of three letters to him—letters pathetically eager and pleading, in which the writer calls herself "Daisy" and the recipient "Master"—were found among Emily Dickinson's papers after her death.

Whether Wadsworth responded to, or was alarmed by, the intensity of the emotion he inspired, as evidenced by these drafts and by certain of her poems, cannot be determined, since his letters were destroyed. But it is known that he called on her in 1860, while visiting a friend in nearby Northampton. And it is conjectured that sometime during the following year he told her that soon he would have "left the land," having accepted a call to a church in San Francisco. The shock of separation may account for the prodigious output of 1862. "I had a terror since September, I could tell to none," she wrote in that year, "and so I sing, as the boy does by the burying ground, because I am afraid." And this is the loss to which the last two lines of the poem quoted above must refer:

Angels, twice descending,
Reimbursed my store.
Burglar, banker, father,
I am poor once more!

As George F. Whicher said in his excellent biography, *This Was a Poet,* "Her dream-palace was suddenly left tenantless."

In that same year Emily Dickinson seems to have considered, for the first time, the possibility of publication, for she sent four poems to Thomas Wentworth Higginson, a rising young man of letters, with a note asking him to "say if my verse is alive." The correspondence and interview that followed so illuminate Emily Dickinson, both as poet and as person, that Higginson's essay on the subject is reprinted in this volume.

If one may think of the first decade of Emily Dickinson's adult life as a period of expansion to the creative climax of 1862, then the remaining years marked a gradual retreat. Year by year the area of her interests narrowed; year by year her indifference to the outer world grew more arctic. Now she dressed only in white; ventured less and less, and finally not at all, from her home; saw fewer friends, and, at last, none. But with one curious exception. Judge Otis P. Lord of Salem, a widower in his late sixties and an old family friend, visited Amherst often during these years, and it would appear—on the evidence of surviving drafts of fifteen letters written between 1878 and 1883—that she conceived for him a passionate love, and even hoped for marriage.

In these last years Emily Dickinson tended her garden, baked the family's bread, and watched from her window the passing show of village life. To her friends she sent gifts of flowers with gnomic notes and poems which vastly puzzled them. She grew obsessed with death, and as her friends departed to "that bareheaded life under the grass" she condoled with the bereaved in letters that are morbidly curious. Long before her death she had become an Amherst legend: the woman in white; the eccentric recluse; the half-cracked daughter of Squire Dickinson.

How closely Emily Dickinson had guarded her writing, even from her immediate family, is shown by her sister's astonishment at coming upon a locked box filled with poems. She had already burned, unread, Emily's correspondence, but these poems, the work of her dear sister, must be given to the world. First she turned to Sue Dickinson, Austin's wife, but the task was difficult and Sue was indolent. Next Lavinia solicited Mabel Loomis Todd, the brilliant young wife of an Amherst professor. Reluctantly Mrs. Todd consented to undertake the long labor of deciphering the handwriting, copying the poems, and selecting enough for a slim volume. With the help of Thomas Wentworth Higginson she finished the task and found a publisher who agreed to bring out the book if the family would pay part of the cost. It appeared in 1890, and was followed by two others and by two volumes of letters. More poems were published in 1914, and again during the twenties, when their place in literature was at last recognized. Finally, in 1950, Harvard University bought all available manuscripts and publishing rights, and has since issued the complete poems and letters, each in three large volumes, edited by Thomas H. Johnson; an edition that cannot be too highly recommended to those who desire to explore further her life and work.

The Anchor Edition of *Selected Poems and Letters of Emily Dickinson* is designed for readers who wish to have in one volume the best of her poetry and the most interesting of her letters. As is inevitable for a poet who worked in solitude and without criticism, her writing is uneven, sometimes baffling in its concision, sometimes provoking in its disregard of rhymes and rules. But at her best she writes as Thoreau wished to live—close to the bone, concentrating the very essence of what she saw and felt in phrases that strike and penetrate like bullets, and with an originality of thought unsurpassed in American poetry.

Robert N. Linscott

Emily Dickinson

THOMAS WENTWORTH HIGGINSON

*I find ecstasy in living; the mere sense of
living is joy enough.*

In 1862, Thomas Wentworth Higginson, a Unitarian clergy-man, contributed to the *Atlantic Monthly* a "Letter" of encouragement and advice to the young writers of America. Shortly after, he received from Amherst, Massachusetts, four poems with a letter asking him to "say if my verse is alive." The letter was unsigned, but enclosed with it was a card on which "Emily Dickinson" was lightly penciled. Thus began what is, perhaps, the most provocative correspondence in the history of American literature.

That same year, Higginson enlisted in the Union army. After the war he settled in Newport, Rhode Island, and became a writer and lecturer. Meanwhile the correspondence with Emily Dickinson had continued, and in 1870, after repeated invitations, he visited "my eccentric poetess" in Amherst. Twenty years later, and four years after Emily's death, he assisted Mabel Loomis Todd in editing her poems; and the following year he contributed to the *Atlantic Monthly* an article in which he quoted some of her letters and poems and described the impression that she had made upon him on the occasion of his visit, now invaluable as the only contemporary and full-length delineation of Emily Dickinson that we have.

If Higginson had been more discerning and less timidly conventional, if he had had the ability to recognize genius in a new and original form, and the courage to sponsor it and to urge publication, it is possible that Emily Dickinson would have found fame in her lifetime, broken free from her cloistered existence, and discovered other—though not, perhaps, more effective—techniques of self-expression.

This is speculation. The fact is that, although she disregarded his somewhat patronizing advice, she found in Higginson a fellow writer who served throughout her life as a literary companion and sounding board. He could not inspire her as a poet, but he could inspire her most impish and illuminating letters.

In the following pages Higginson's *Atlantic* essay is reprinted, slightly abridged, and with the omission of most of the poems he quoted since these are printed in the body of this book.

. . . On April 16, 1862, I took from the post-office the following letter:—

Mr. Higginson,—Are you too deeply occupied to say if my verse is alive?

The mind is so near itself it cannot see distinctly, and I have none to ask.

Should you think it breathed, and had you the leisure to tell me, I should feel quick gratitude.

If I make the mistake, that you dared to tell me would give me sincerer honor toward you.

I inclose my name, asking you, if you please, sir, to tell me what is true?

That you will not betray me it is needless to ask, since honor is its own pawn.

The letter was postmarked "Amherst," and it was in a handwriting so peculiar that it seemed as if the writer might have taken her first lessons by studying the famous fossil bird-tracks in the museum of that college town. Yet it was not in the slightest degree illiterate, but cultivated, quaint, and wholly unique. Of punctuation there was little; she used chiefly dashes, and it has been thought better, in printing these letters, as with her poems, to give them the benefit in this respect of the ordinary usages; and so with her habit as to capitalization, as the printers call it, in which she followed the Old English and present German method of thus distin-

5

guishing every noun substantive. But the most curious thing about the letter was the total absence of a signature. It proved, however, that she had written her name on a card, and put it under the shelter of a smaller envelope inclosed in the larger; and even this name was written—as if the shy writer wished to recede as far as possible from view—in pencil, not in ink. The name was Emily Dickinson. Inclosed with the letter were four poems, two of which have since been separately printed,—"Safe in their alabaster chambers" and "I'll tell you how the sun rose." . . .

The impression of a wholly new and original poetic genius was as distinct on my mind at the first reading of these four poems as it is now, after half a century of further knowledge; and with it came the problem never yet solved, what place ought to be assigned in literature to what is so remarkable, yet so elusive of criticism. The bee himself did not evade the schoolboy more than she evaded me; and even at this day I still stand somewhat bewildered, like the boy.

Circumstances, however, soon brought me in contact with an uncle of Emily Dickinson, a gentleman not now living: a prominent citizen of Worcester, Massachusetts, a man of integrity and character, who shared her abruptness and impulsiveness, but certainly not her poetic temperament, from which he was indeed singularly remote. He could tell but little of her, she being evidently an enigma to him, as to me. It is hard to say what answer was made by me, under these circumstances, to this letter. It is probable that the adviser sought to gain time a little and find out with what strange creature he was dealing. I remember to have ventured on some criticism which she afterwards called "surgery," and on some questions, part of which she evaded, as will be seen, with a naïve skill such as the most experienced and worldly coquette might envy. Her second letter (received April 26, 1862) was as follows:—

Mr. Higginson,—Your kindness claimed earlier gratitude, but I was ill, and write to-day from my pillow.

Thank you for the surgery; it was not so painful as I supposed. I bring you others, as you ask, though they might not differ. While my thought is undressed, I can make the distinction; but when I put them in the gown, they look alike and numb.

You asked how old I was? I made no verse, but one or two, until this winter, sir.

I had a terror since September, I could tell to none; and so I sing, as the boy does by the burying ground, because I am afraid.

You inquire my books. For poets, I have Keats, and Mr. and Mrs. Browning. For prose, Mr. Ruskin, Sir Thomas Browne, and the Revelations. I went to school, but in your manner of the phrase had no education. When a little girl, I had a friend who taught me Immortality; but venturing too near, himself, he never returned. Soon after my tutor died, and for several years my lexicon was my only companion. Then I found one more, but he was not contented I be his scholar, so he left the land.

You ask of my companions. Hills, sir, and the sundown, and a dog large as myself, that my father bought me. They are better than beings because they know, but do not tell; and the noise in the pool at noon excels my piano.

I have a brother and sister; my mother does not care for thought, and father, too busy with his briefs to notice what we do. He buys me many books, but begs me not to read them, because he fears they joggle the mind. They are religious, except me, and address an eclipse, every morning, whom they call their "Father."

But I fear my story fatigues you. I would like to learn. Could you tell me how to grow, or is it unconveyed, like melody or witchcraft?

You speak of Mr. Whitman. I never read his book, but was told that it was disgraceful.

I read Miss Prescott's "Circumstance," but it followed me in the dark, so I avoided her.

Two editors of journals came to my father's house this winter, and asked me for my mind, and when I asked them "why" they said I was penurious, and they would use it for the world.

I could not weigh myself, myself. My size felt small to

me. I read your chapters in the "Atlantic," and experienced honor for you. I was sure you would not reject a confiding question.

Is this, sir, what you asked me to tell you? Your friend,
E. Dickinson

It will be seen that she had now drawn a step nearer, signing her name, and as my "friend." It will also be noticed that I had sounded her about certain American authors, then much read; and that she knew how to put her own criticisms in a very trenchant way. With this letter came some more verses, still in the same birdlike script. . . .

It is possible that in a second letter I gave more of distinct praise or encouragement, as her third is in a different mood. This was received June 8, 1862. There is something startling in its opening image; and in the yet stranger phrase that follows, where she apparently uses "mob" in the sense of chaos or bewilderment:

Dear Friend,—Your letter gave no drunkenness, because I tasted rum before. Domingo comes but once; yet I have had few pleasures so deep as your opinion, and if I tried to thank you, my tears would block my tongue.

My dying tutor told me that he would like to live till I had been a poet, but Death was much of mob as I could master, then. And when, far afterward, a sudden light on orchards, or a new fashion in the wind troubled my attention, I felt a palsy, here, the verses just relieve.

Your second letter surprised me, and for a moment, swung. I had not supposed it. Your first gave no dishonor, because the true are not ashamed. I thanked you for your justice, but could not drop the bells whose jingling cooled my tramp. Perhaps the balm seemed better, because you bled me first. I smile when you suggest that I delay "to publish," that being foreign to my thought as firmament to fin.

If fame belonged to me, I could not escape her; if she did not, the longest day would pass me on the chase, and the approbation of my dog would forsake me then. My barefoot rank is better.

You think my gait "spasmodic." I am in danger, sir. You think me "uncontrolled." I have no tribunal.

Would you have time to be the "friend" you should think I need? I have a little shape: it would not crowd your desk, nor make much racket as the mouse that dens your galleries.

If I might bring you what I do—not so frequent to trouble you—and ask you if I told it clear, 't would be control to me. The sailor cannot see the North, but knows the needle can. The "hand you stretch me in the dark" I put mine in, and turn away. I have no Saxon now:—

As if I asked a common alms,
And in my wandering hand
A stranger pressed a kingdom,
And I, bewildered, stand;
As if I asked the Orient
Had it for me a morn,
And it should lift its purple dikes
And shatter me with dawn!

But, will you be my preceptor, Mr. Higginson?

With this came the poem since published in one of her volumes and entitled "Renunciation"; and also that beginning "Of all the sounds dispatched abroad," thus fixing approximately the date of those two. I must soon have written to ask her for her picture, that I might form some impression of my enigmatical correspondent. To this came the following reply, in July, 1862:—

Could you believe me without? I had no portrait, now, but am small, like the wren; and my hair is bold like the chestnut bur; and my eyes, like the sherry in the glass, that the guest leaves. Would this do just as well?

It often alarms father. He says death might occur and he has moulds of all the rest, but has no mould of me; but I noticed the quick wore off those things, in a few days, and forestall the dishonor. You will think no caprice of me.

You said "Dark." I know the butterfly, and the lizard, and the orchis. Are not those *your* countrymen?

I am happy to be your scholar, and will deserve the kindness I cannot repay.

If you truly consent, I recite now. Will you tell me my fault, frankly as to yourself, for I had rather wince than die. Men do not call the surgeon to commend the bone, but to set it, sir, and fracture within is more critical. And for this, preceptor, I shall bring you obedience, the blossom from my garden, and every gratitude I know.

Perhaps you smile at me. I could not stop for that. My business is circumference. An ignorance, not of customs, but if caught with the dawn, or the sunset see me, myself the only kangaroo among the beauty, sir, if you please, it afflicts me, and I thought that instruction would take it away.

Because you have much business, beside the growth of me, you will appoint, yourself, how often I shall come, without your inconvenience.

And if at any time you regret you received me, or I prove a different fabric to that you supposed, you must banish me.

When I state myself, as the representative of the verse, it does not mean me, but a supposed person.

You are true about the "perfection." To-day makes Yesterday mean.

You spoke of "Pippa Passes." I never heard anybody speak of "Pippa Passes" before. You see my posture is benighted.

To thank you baffles me. Are you perfectly powerful? Had I a pleasure you had not, I could delight to bring it.

Your Scholar

It would seem that at first I tried a little—a very little—to lead her in the direction of rules and traditions; but I fear it was only perfunctory, and that she interested me more in her —so to speak—unregenerate condition. Still, she recognized the endeavor. In this case, as will be seen, I called her attention to the fact that while she took pains to correct the spelling of a word, she was utterly careless of greater irregularities. It will be seen by her answer that with her usual naïve adroitness she turns my point:—

Dear Friend,—Are these more orderly? I thank you for the truth.

I had no monarch in my life, and cannot rule myself; and when I try to organize, my little force explodes and leaves me bare and charred.

I think you called me "wayward." Will you help me improve?

I suppose the pride that stops the breath, in the core of woods, is not of ourself.

You say I confess the little mistake, and omit the large. Because I can see orthography; but the ignorance out of sight is my preceptor's charge.

Of "shunning men and women," they talk of hallowed things, aloud, and embarrass my dog. He and I don't object to them, if they'll exist their side. I think Carlo would please you. He is dumb, and brave. I think you would like the chestnut tree I met in my walk. It hit my notice suddenly, and I thought the skies were in blossom.

Then there's a noiseless noise in the orchard that I let persons hear.

You told me in one letter you could not come to see me "now," and I made no answer; not because I had none, but did not think myself the price that you should come so far.

I do not ask so large a pleasure, lest you might deny me.

You say, "Beyond your knowledge." You would not jest with me, because I believe you; but, preceptor, you cannot mean it?

All men say "What" to me, but I thought it a fashion.

When much in the woods, as a little girl, I was told that the snake would bite me, that I might pick a poisonous flower, or goblins kidnap me; but I went along and met no one but angels, who were far shyer of me than I could be of them, so I haven't that confidence in fraud which many exercise.

I shall observe your precept, though I don't understand it, always.

I marked a line in one verse, because I met it after I made it, and never consciously touch a paint mixed by another person.

I do not let go it, because it is mine. Have you the portrait of Mrs. Browning?

Persons sent me three. If you had none, will you have mine?

Your Scholar

A month or two after this I entered the volunteer army of the Civil War, and must have written to her during the winter of 1862–63 from South Carolina or Florida, for the following reached me in camp:—

Amherst

Dear Friend,—I did not deem that planetary forces annulled, but suffered an exchange of territory, or world.

I should have liked to see you before you became improbable. War feels to me an oblique place. Should there be other summers, would you perhaps come?

I found you were gone, by accident, as I find systems are, or seasons of the year, and obtain no cause, but suppose it a treason of progress that dissolves as it goes. Carlo still remained, and I told him.

Best gains must have the losses' test,
To constitute them gains.

My shaggy ally assented.

Perhaps death gave me awe for friends, striking sharp and early, for I held them since in a brittle love, of more alarm than peace. I trust you may pass the limit of war; and though not reared to prayer, when service is had in church for our arms, I include yourself. . . . I was thinking to-day, as I noticed, that the "Supernatural" was only the Natural disclosed.

> Not "Revelation" 't is that waits,
> But our unfurnished eyes.

But I fear I detain you. Should you, before this reaches you, experience immortality, who will inform me of the exchange? Could you, with honor, avoid death, I entreat you, sir. It would bereave

Your Gnome

I trust the "Procession of Flowers" was not a premonition.

I cannot explain this extraordinary signature, substituted for the now customary "Your Scholar," unless she imagined her friend to be in some incredible and remote condition, imparting its strangeness to her. Swedenborg somewhere has an image akin to her "oblique place," where he symbolizes evil as simply an oblique angle. With this letter came verses, most refreshing in that clime of jasmines and mockingbirds, on the familiar robin.

In the summer of 1863 I was wounded, and in hospital for a time, during which came this letter in pencil, written from what was practically a hospital for her, though only for weak eyes:—

Dear Friend,—Are you in danger? I did not know that you were hurt. Will you tell me more? Mr. Hawthorne died.

I was ill since September, and since April in Boston for a physician's care. He does not let me go, yet I work in my prison, and make guests for myself.

Carlo did not come, because that he would die in jail; and the mountains I could not hold now, so I brought but the Gods.

I wish to see you more than before I failed. Will you tell me your health? I am surprised and anxious since receiving your note.

The only news I know
Is bulletins all day
From Immortality.

Can you render my pencil? The physician has taken away my pen.

I inclose the address from a letter, lest my figures fail.

Knowledge of your recovery would excel my own.

E. Dickinson

Later this arrived:—

Dear Friend,—I think of you so wholly that I cannot resist to write again, to ask if you are safe? Danger is not at first, for then we are unconscious, but in the after, slower days.

Do not try to be saved, but let redemption find you, as it certainly will. Love is its own rescue; for we, at our supremest, are but its trembling emblems.

Your Scholar

These were my earliest letters from Emily Dickinson, in their order. From this time and up to her death (May 15, 1886) we corresponded at varying intervals, she always persistently keeping up this attitude of "Scholar," and assuming on my part a preceptorship which it is almost needless to say did not exist. Always glad to hear her "recite," as she called it, I soon abandoned all attempt to guide in the slightest degree this extraordinary nature, and simply accepted her confidences, giving as much as I could of what might interest her in return.

Sometimes there would be a long pause, on my part, after which would come a plaintive letter, always terse, like this:—

"Did I displease you? But won't you tell me how?"

Or perhaps the announcement of some event, vast in her small sphere, as this:—

Amherst
E. Dickinson

Carlo died.
Would you instruct me now?

Or sometimes there would arrive an exquisite little detached strain, every word a picture, like this:—

THE HUMMING-BIRD
A route of evanescence
With a revolving wheel;
A resonance of emerald;
A rush of cochineal.
And every blossom on the bush
Adjusts its tumbled head;—
The mail from Tunis, probably,
An easy morning's ride.

Nothing in literature, I am sure, so condenses into a few words that gorgeous atom of life and fire of which she here attempts the description. It is, however, needless to conceal that many of her brilliant fragments were less satisfying. She almost always grasped whatever she sought, but with some fracture of grammar and dictionary on the way. Often, too, she was obscure, and sometimes inscrutable; and though obscurity is sometimes, in Coleridge's phrase, a compliment to the reader, yet it is never safe to press this compliment too hard.

Sometimes, on the other hand, her verses found too much favor for her comfort, and she was urged to publish. In such cases I was sometimes put forward as a defense; and the following letter was the fruit of some such occasion:

Dear Friend,—Thank you for the advice. I shall implicitly follow it.

The one who asked me for the lines I had never seen.

He spoke of "a charity." I refused, but did not inquire. He again earnestly urged, on the ground that in that way I might "aid unfortunate children." The name of "child" was a snare to me, and I hesitated, choosing my most rudimentary, and without criterion.

I inquired of you. You can scarcely estimate the opinion to one utterly guideless. Again thank you.

Your Scholar

Again came this, on a similar theme:—

Dear Friend,—Are you willing to tell me what is right? Mrs. Jackson, of Colorado ["H. H.," her early school-mate], was with me a few moments this week, and wished me to write for this. [A circular of the "No Name Series" was inclosed.] I told her I was unwilling, and she asked me why? I said I was incapable, and she seemed not to believe me and asked me not to decide for a few days. Meantime, she would write me. She was so sweetly noble, I would regret to estrange her, and if you would be willing to give me a note saying you disapproved it, and thought me unfit, she would believe you. I am sorry to flee so often to my safest friend, but hope he permits me.

In all this time—nearly eight years—we had never met, but she had sent invitations like the following:—

Amherst

Dear Friend,—Whom my dog understood could not elude others.

I should be so glad to see you, but think it an appari-tional pleasure, not to be fulfilled. I am uncertain of Bos-ton.

I had promised to visit my physician for a few days in May, but father objects because he is in the habit of me.

Is it more far to Amherst?

You will find a minute host, but a spacious wel-come. . . .

If I still entreat you to teach me, are you much dis-pleased? I will be patient, constant, never reject your knife, and should my slowness goad you, you knew before my-self that

Except the smaller size
No lives are round.
These hurry to a sphere
And show and end.
The larger slower grow
And later hang;

The summers of Hesperides
Are long.

Afterwards, came this:—

                                    Amherst
Dear Friend,—A letter always feels to me like immortality because it is the mind alone without corporeal friend. Indebted in our talk to attitude and accent, there seems a spectral power in thought that walks alone. I would like to thank you for your great kindness, but never try to lift the words which I cannot hold.

Should you come to Amherst, I might then succeed, though gratitude is the timid wealth of those who have nothing. I am sure that you speak the truth, because the noble do, but your letters always surprise me.

My life has been too simple and stern to embarrass any. "Seen of Angels," scarcely my responsibility.

It is difficult not to be fictitious in so fair a place, but tests' severe repairs are permitted all.

When a little girl I remember hearing that remarkable passage and preferring the "Power," not knowing at the time that "Kingdom" and "Glory" were included.

You noticed my dwelling alone. To an emigrant, country is idle except it be his own. You speak kindly of seeing me; could it please your convenience to come so far as Amherst, I should be very glad, but I do not cross my father's ground to any house or town.

Of our greatest acts we are ignorant. You were not aware that you saved my life. To thank you in person has been since then one of my few requests. . . . You will excuse each that I say, because no one taught me.

At last, after many postponements, on August 16, 1870, I found myself face to face with my hitherto unseen correspondent. It was at her father's house, one of those large, square, brick mansions so familiar in our older New England towns, surrounded by trees and blossoming shrubs without, and within exquisitely neat, cool, spacious, and fragrant with flowers. After a little delay, I heard an extremely faint and

17

pattering footstep like that of a child, in the hall, and in glided, almost noiselessly, a plain, shy little person, the face without a single good feature, but with eyes, as she herself said, "like the sherry the guest leaves in the glass," and with smooth bands of reddish chestnut hair. She had a quaint and nun-like look, as if she might be a German canoness of some religious order, whose prescribed garb was white piqué, with a blue net worsted shawl. She came toward me with two day-lilies, which she put in a childlike way into my hand, saying softly, under her breath, "These are my introduction," and adding, also under her breath, in childlike fashion, "Forgive me if I am frightened; I never see strangers, and hardly know what I say." But soon she began to talk, and thenceforward continued almost constantly; pausing sometimes to beg that I would talk instead, but readily recommencing when I evaded. There was not a trace of affectation in all this; she seemed to speak absolutely for her own relief, and wholly without watching its effect on her hearer. Led on by me, she told much about her early life, in which her father was always the chief figure,—evidently a man of the old type, *la vieille roche* of Puritanism,—a man who, as she said, read on Sunday "lonely and rigorous books"; and who had from childhood inspired her with such awe, that she never learned to tell time by the clock till she was fifteen, simply because he had tried to explain it to her when she was a little child, and she had been afraid to tell him that she did not understand, and also afraid to ask any one else lest he should hear of it. Yet she had never heard him speak a harsh word, and it needed only a glance at his photograph to see how truly the Puritan tradition was preserved in him. He did not wish his children, when little, to read anything but the Bible; and when, one day, her brother brought her home Longfellow's "Kavanagh," he put it secretly under the pianoforte cover, made signs to her, and they both afterwards read it. It may have been before this, however, that a student of her father's was amazed to find that she and her brother had never heard of Lydia Maria Child, then much read, and he brought "Letters from New York," and hid it in the great bush of old-fashioned tree-box beside the front door. After the first book, she thought in ecstasy, "This, then, is a book, and there are more of them." But she did not find so many as she expected, for she afterwards said to me, "When I lost the use of my eyes, it was a comfort to think that there were so few real books that I could easily find one to read me all of them." Afterwards, when she regained her eyes, she read Shakespeare, and thought to herself, "Why is any other book needed?"

She went on talking constantly and saying, in the midst of narrative, things quaint and aphoristic. "Is it oblivion or absorption when things pass from our minds?" "Truth is such a rare thing, it is delightful to tell it." "I find ecstasy in living; the mere sense of living is joy enough." When I asked her if she never felt any want of employment, not going off the grounds and rarely seeing a visitor, she answered, "I never thought of conceiving that I could ever have the slightest approach to such a want in all future time"; and then added, after a pause, "I feel that I have not expressed myself strongly enough," although it seemed to me that she had. She told me of her household occupations, that she made all their bread, because her father liked only hers; then saying shyly, "And people must have puddings," this very timidly and suggestively, as if they were meteors or comets. Interspersed with these confidences came phrases so emphasized as to seem the very wantonness of over-statement, as if she pleased herself with putting into words what the most extravagant might possibly think without saying, as thus: "How do most people live without any thoughts? There are many people in the world,—you must have noticed them in the street,—how do they live? How do they get strength to put on their clothes in the morning?" Or this crowning extravaganza: "If I read a book and it makes my whole body so cold no fire can ever warm me, I know that is poetry. If I feel physically as if the top of my head were taken off, I know that is poetry. These are the only ways I know it. Is there any other way?"

I have tried to describe her just as she was, with the aid of notes taken at the time; but this interview left our relation very much what it was before;—on my side an interest that was strong and even affectionate, but not based on any thorough comprehension; and on her side a hope, always rather baffled, that I should afford some aid in solving her abstruse problem of life.

The impression undoubtedly made on me was that of an excess of tension, and of something abnormal. Perhaps in time I could have got beyond that somewhat overstrained relation which not my will, but her needs, had forced upon us. Certainly I should have been most glad to bring it down to the level of simple truth and every-day comradeship; but it was not altogether easy. She was much too enigmatical a being for me to solve in an hour's interview, and an instinct told me that the slightest attempt at direct cross-examination would make her withdraw into her shell; I could only sit still and watch, as one does in the woods; I must name my bird without a gun, as recommended by Emerson.

After my visit came this letter:—

Enough is so vast a sweetness, I suppose it never occurs, only pathetic counterfeits.

Fabulous to me as the men of the Revelations who "shall not hunger any more." Even the possible has its insoluble particle.

After you went, I took "Macbeth" and turned to "Birnam Wood." Came twice "To Dunsinane." I thought and went about my work. . . .

The vein cannot thank the artery, but her solemn indebtedness to him, even the stolidest admit, and so of me who try, whose effort leaves no sound.

You ask great questions accidentally. To answer them would be events. I trust that you are safe.

I ask you to forgive me for all the ignorance I had. I find no nomination sweet as your low opinion.

Speak, if but to blame your obedient child.

You told me of Mrs. Lowell's poems. Would you tell me where I could find them, or are they not for sight? An article of yours, too, perhaps the only one you wrote that I never knew. It was about a "Latch." Are you willing to tell me? [Perhaps "A Sketch."]

If I ask too much, you could please refuse. Shortness to live has made me bold.

Abroad is close to-night and I have but to lift my hands to touch the "Heights of Abraham."

Dickinson

When I said, at parting, that I would come again some time, she replied, "Say, in a long time; that will be nearer. Some time is no time." We met only once again, and I have no express record of the visit. We corresponded for years, at long intervals, her side of the intercourse being, I fear, better sustained; and she sometimes wrote also to my wife, inclosing flowers or fragrant leaves with a verse or two. Once she sent her one of George Eliot's books, I think "Middlemarch," and wrote, "I am bringing you a little granite book for you to lean upon." At other times she would send single poems.

Then came the death of her father, that strong Puritan father who had communicated to her so much of the vigor of his own nature, and who bought her many books, but begged her not to read them. Mr. Edward Dickinson, after service in the national House of Representatives and other public positions, had become a member of the lower house of the Massachusetts legislature. The session was unusually prolonged, and he was making a speech upon some railway question at noon, one very hot day (June 15, 1874), when he became suddenly faint and sat down. The house adjourned, and a friend walked with him to his lodgings at the Tremont House, where he began to pack his bag for home, after sending for a physician, but died within three hours. Soon afterwards, I received the following letter:—

The last afternoon that my father lived, though with no premonition, I preferred to be with him, and invented an absence for mother, Vinnie [her sister] being asleep. He seemed peculiarly pleased, as I oftenest stayed with myself; and remarked, as the afternoon withdrew, he "would like it to not end."

His pleasure almost embarrassed me, and my brother coming, I suggested they walk. Next morning I woke him for the train, and saw him no more.

His heart was pure and terrible, and I think no other like it exists.

I am glad there is immortality, but would have tested it myself, before entrusting him. Mr. Bowles was with us. With that exception, I saw none. I have wished for you, since my father died, and had you an hour unengrossed, it would be almost priceless. Thank you for each kindness. . . .

Later she wrote:—

When I think of my father's lonely life and lonelier death, there is this redress—

Take all away;
The only thing worth larceny
Is left—the immortality.

My earliest friend wrote me the week before he died, "If I live, I will go to Amherst; if I die, I certainly will."
Is your house deeper off?

Your Scholar

A year afterwards came this:—

Dear Friend,—Mother was paralyzed Tuesday, a year from the evening father died. I thought perhaps you would care.

Your Scholar

With this came the following verse, having a curious seventeenth-century flavor:—

"A death-blow is a life-blow to some,
  Who, till they died, did not alive become;
  Who, had they lived, had died, but when
  They died, vitality begun."

And later came this kindred memorial of one of the oldest and most faithful friends of the family, Mr. Samuel Bowles, of the Springfield "Republican":—

Dear Friend,—I felt it shelter to speak to you.

My brother and sister are with Mr. Bowles, who is buried this afternoon.

The last song that I heard—that was, since the birds—was "He leadeth me, he leadeth me; yea, though I walk"—then the voices stooped, the arch was so low.

After this added bereavement the inward life of the diminished household became only more concentrated, and the world was held farther and farther away. Yet to this period belongs the following letter, written about 1880, which has more of what is commonly called the objective or external quality than any she ever wrote me; and shows how close might have been her observation and her sympathy, had her rare qualities taken a somewhat different channel:—

Dear Friend,—I was touchingly reminded of [a child who had died] this morning by an Indian woman with gay baskets and a dazzling baby, at the kitchen door. Her little boy "once died," she said, death to her dispelling him. I asked her what the baby liked, and she said "to step." The prairie before the door was gay with flowers of hay, and I led her in. She argued with the birds, she leaned on clover walls and they fell, and dropped her. With jargon sweeter than a bell, she grappled buttercups, and they sank together, the buttercups the heaviest. What sweetest use of days! 'T was noting some such scene made Vaughan humbly say,—

"My days that are at best but dim and hoary."

I think it was Vaughan. . . .

And these few fragmentary memorials—closing, like every human biography, with funerals, yet with such as were to Emily Dickinson only the stately introduction to a higher life

—may well end with her description of the death of the very summer she so loved.

"As imperceptibly as grief
  The summer lapsed away,
  Too imperceptible at last
  To feel like perfidy.

"A quietness distilled,
  As twilight long begun,
  Or Nature spending with herself
  Sequestered afternoon.

"The dusk drew earlier in,
  The morning foreign shone,
  A courteous yet harrowing grace
  As guest that would be gone.

"And thus without a wing
  Or service of a keel
  Our summer made her light escape
  Into the Beautiful."

Selected Poems

My business is circumference.

Emily Dickinson wrote in all seventeen hundred and seventy-five poems, of which only seven were published in her lifetime, all anonymously. The poems were undated and, with the exception of twenty-four, untitled. All but one hundred and twenty-three of the published poems still exist in her own handwriting. These can be approximately dated by the script, which changed strikingly decade by decade and almost year by year.

The poems that follow are arranged by years in some approximation to chronological order, except for the last seventeen, which cannot be dated since they exist only in copies.

The test used follows the text of the volumes printed in 1890, 1891, and 1896. In these early editions Emily Dickinson's erratic punctuation and lavish use of capital letters were changed to conform to accepted usage, and occasional liberties were taken with the text in order to correct grammatical vagaries or to clarify rhyme or meaning. Scholars who wish to study the exact original text should consult the three-volume edition mentioned in the Introduction.

I never lost as much but twice,
And that was in the sod;
Twice have I stood a beggar
Before the door of God!

Angels, twice descending,
Reimbursed my store.
Burglar, banker, father,
I am poor once more!

———

On this wondrous sea,
  Sailing silently,
  Ho! pilot, ho!
Knowest thou the shore
Where no breakers roar,
  Where the storm is o'er?

In the silent west
Many sails at rest,
  Their anchors fast;
Thither I pilot thee,—
Land, ho! Eternity!
  Ashore at last!

———

The morns are meeker than they were,
The nuts are getting brown;
The berry's cheek is plumper,
The rose is out of town.

The maple wears a gayer scarf,
The field a scarlet gown.
Lest I should be old-fashioned,
I'll put a trinket on.

———

The gentian weaves her fringes,
The maple's loom is red.
My departing blossoms
Obviate parade.

A brief, but patient illness,
An hour to prepare;
And one, below this morning,
Is where the angels are.

It was a short procession,—
The bobolink was there,
An aged bee addressed us,
And then we knelt in prayer.

We trust that she was willing,—
We ask that we may be.
Summer, sister, seraph,
Let us go with thee!

In the name of the bee
And of the butterfly
And of the breeze, amen!

———

Frequently the woods arc pink,
Frequently are brown;
Frequently the hills undress
Behind my native town.

Oft a head is crested
I was wont to see,
And as oft a cranny
Where it used to be.

And the earth, they tell me,
On its axis turned,—
Wonderful rotation
By but twelve performed!

———

Sleep is supposed to be,
By souls of sanity,
The shutting of the eye.

Sleep is the station grand
Down which on either hand
The hosts of witness stand!

Morn is supposed to be,
By people of degree,
The breaking of the day.

Morning has not occurred!
That shall aurora be
East of eternity;

One with the banner gay,
One in the red array,—
That is the break of day.

———

Morns like these we parted;
Noons like these she rose,
Fluttering first, then firmer,
To her fair repose.

Never did she lisp it,
And 'twas not for me;
She was mute from transport,
I, from agony!

Till the evening, nearing,
One the shutters drew—
Quick! a sharper rustling!
And this linnet flew!

———

I had a guinea golden;
    I lost it in the sand,
And though the sum was simple,
    And pounds were in the land,
Still had it such a value
    Unto my frugal eye,
That when I could not find it
    I sat me down to sigh.

I had a crimson robin
    Who sang full many a day,
But when the woods were painted
    He, too, did fly away.
Time brought me other robins,—
    Their ballads were the same,—
Still for my missing troubadour
    I kept the "house at hame."

I had a star in heaven;
    One Pleiad was its name,
And when I was not heeding
    It wandered from the same.

And though the skies are crowded,
    And all the night ashine,
I do not care about it,
    Since none of them are mine.

My story has a moral:
    I have a missing friend,—
Pleiad its name, and robin,
    And guinea in the sand,—
And when this mournful ditty,
    Accompanied with tear,
Shall meet the eye of traitor
    In country far from here,
Grant that repentance solemn
    May seize upon his mind,
And he no consolation
    Beneath the sun may find.

———

It's all I have to bring to-day,
    This, and my heart beside,
This, and my heart, and all the fields,
    And all the meadows wide.
Be sure you count, should I forget,—
    Some one the sum could tell,—
This, and my heart, and all the bees
    Which in the clover dwell.

———

When roses cease to bloom, dear,
    And violets are done,
When bumble-bees in solemn flight
    Have passed beyond the sun,

The hand that paused to gather
    Upon this summer's day
Will idle lie, in Auburn,—
    Then take my flower, pray!

————

Who robbed the woods,
The trusting woods?
The unsuspecting trees
Brought out their burrs and mosses
His fantasy to please.
He scanned their trinkets, curious,
He grasped, he bore away.
What will the solemn hemlock,
What will the fir-tree say?

————

Before the ice is in the pools,
    Before the skaters go,
Or any cheek at nightfall
    Is tarnished by the snow,

Before the fields have finished,
    Before the Christmas tree,
Wonder upon wonder
    Will arrive to me!

What we touch the hems of
    On a summer's day;
What is only walking
    Just a bridge away;

That which sings so, speaks so,
    When there's no one here,—
Will the frock I wept in
    Answer me to wear?

——

Summer for thee grant I may be
    When summer days are flown!
Thy music still when whippoorwill
    And oriole are done!

For thee to bloom, I'll skip the tomb
    And sow my blossoms o'er!
Pray gather me, Anemone,
    Thy flower forevermore!

——

There's something quieter than sleep
    Within this inner room!
It wears a sprig upon its breast,
    And will not tell its name.

Some touch it and some kiss it,
    Some chafe its idle hand;
It has a simple gravity
    I do not understand!

While simple-hearted neighbors
    Chat of the "early dead,"
We, prone to periphrasis,
    Remark that birds have fled!

——

If I should die,
And you should live,
And time should gurgle on,
And morn should beam,
And noon should burn,
As it has usual done;
If birds should build as early,
And bees as bustling go,—
One might depart at option
From enterprise below!
'Tis sweet to know that stocks will stand
When we with daisies lie,
That commerce will continue,
And trades as briskly fly.
It makes the parting tranquil
And keeps the soul serene,
That gentlemen so sprightly
Conduct the pleasing scene!

———

I have not told my garden yet,
Lest that should conquer me;
I have not quite the strength now
To break it to the bee.

I will not name it in the street,
For shops would stare, that I,
So shy, so very ignorant,
Should have the face to die.

The hillsides must not know it,
Where I have rambled so,
Nor tell the loving forests
The day that I shall go,

Nor lisp it at the table,
Nor heedless by the way
Hint that within the riddle
One will walk to-day!

———

Taken from men this morning,
Carried by men to-day,
Met by the gods with banners
Who marshalled her away.

One little maid from playmates,
One little mind from school,—
There must be guests in Eden;
All the rooms are full.

Far as the east from even,
Dim as the border star,—
Courtiers quaint, in kingdoms,
Our departed are.

———

If recollecting were forgetting,
    Then I remember not;
And if forgetting, recollecting,
    How near I had forgot!
And if to miss were merry,
    And if to mourn were gay,
How very blithe the fingers
    That gathered these to-day!

———

Heart, we will forget him!
   You and I, to-night!
You may forget the warmth he gave,
   I will forget the light.

When you have done, pray tell me,
   That I my thoughts may dim;
Haste! lest while you're lagging,
   I may remember him!

————

Whether my bark went down at sea,
Whether she met with gales,
Whether to isles enchanted
She bent her docile sails;

By what mystic mooring
She is held to-day,—
This is the errand of the eye
Out upon the bay.

————

Success is counted sweetest
By those who ne'er succeed.
To comprehend a nectar
Requires sorest need.

Not one of all the purple host
Who took the flag to-day
Can tell the definition,
So clear, of victory,

As he, defeated, dying,
On whose forbidden ear
The distant strains of triumph
Break, agonized and clear.

———

A throe upon the features,
A hurry in the breath,
An ecstasy of parting
Denominated "Death,"—

An anguish at the mention,
Which, when to patience grown,
I've known permission given
To rejoin its own.

———

Surgeons must be very careful
When they take the knife!
Underneath their fine incisions
Stirs the culprit,—Life!

———

Arcturus is his other name,—
I'd rather call him star!
It's so unkind of science
To go and interfere!

I pull a flower from the woods,—
A monster with a glass
Computes the stamens in a breath,
And has her in a class.

Whereas I took the butterfly
Aforetime in my hat,
He sits erect in cabinets,
The clover-bells forgot.

What once was heaven, is zenith now.
Where I proposed to go
When time's brief masquerade was done,
Is mapped, and charted too!

What if the poles should frisk about
And stand upon their heads!
I hope I'm ready for the worst,
Whatever prank betides!

Perhaps the kingdom of Heaven's changed!
I hope the children there
Won't be new-fashioned when I come,
And laugh at me, and stare!

I hope the father in the skies
Will lift his little girl,—
Old-fashioned, naughty, everything,—
Over the stile of pearl!

————

A lady red upon the hill
    Her annual secret keeps;
A lady white within the field
    In placid lily sleeps!

The tidy breezes with their brooms
    Sweep vale, and hill, and tree!
Prithee, my pretty housewives!
    Who may expected be?

The neighbors do not yet suspect!
  The woods exchange a smile—
Orchard, and buttercup, and bird—
  In such a little while!

And yet how still the landscape stands,
  How nonchalant the wood,
As if the resurrection
  Were nothing very odd!

———

As by the dead we love to sit,
Become so wondrous dear,
As for the lost we grapple,
Though all the rest are here,—

In broken mathematics
We estimate our prize,
Vast, in its fading ratio,
To our penurious eyes!

———

To fight aloud is very brave,
But gallanter, I know,
Who charge within the bosom,
The cavalry of woe.

Who win, and nations do not see,
Who fall, and none observe,
Whose dying eyes no country
Regards with patriot love.

We trust, in plumed procession,
For such the angels go,
Rank after rank, with even feet
And uniforms of snow.

———

The daisy follows soft the sun,
    And when his golden walk is done,
  Sits shyly at his feet.
He, waking, finds the flower near.
"Wherefore, marauder, art thou here?"
  "Because, sir, love is sweet!"

We are the flower, Thou the sun!
Forgive us, if as days decline,
    We nearer steal to Thee,—
Enamoured of the parting west,
The peace, the flight, the amethyst,
    Night's possibility!

———

I have a king who does not speak;
So, wondering, thro' the hours meek
    I trudge the day away,—
Half glad when it is night and sleep,
If, haply, thro' a dream to peep
    In parlors shut by day.

And if I do, when morning comes,
It is as if a hundred drums
    Did round my pillow roll,
And shouts fill all my childish sky,
And bells keep saying "victory"
    From steeples in my soul!

And if I don't, the little bird
Within the orchard is not heard,
    And I omit to pray,
"Father, thy will be done" to-day,
For my will goes the other way,
    And it were perjury!

———

To hang our head ostensibly,
    And subsequent to find
That such was not the posture
    Of our immortal mind,

Affords the sly presumption
    That, in so dense a fuzz,
You, too, take cobweb attitudes
    Upon a plane of gauze!

———

Bring me the sunset in a cup,
Reckon the morning's flagons up,
    And say how many dew;
Tell me how far the morning leaps,
Tell me what time the weaver sleeps
    Who spun the breadths of blue!

Write me how many notes there be
In the new robin's ecstasy
    Among astonished boughs;
How many trips the tortoise makes,
How many cups the bee partakes,—
    The debauchee of dews!

Also, who laid the rainbow's piers,
Also, who leads the docile spheres
    By withes of supple blue?
Whose fingers string the stalactite,
Who counts the wampum of the night,
    To see that none is due?

Who built this little Alban house
And shut the windows down so close
    My spirit cannot see?
Who'll let me out some gala day,
With implements to fly away,
    Passing pomposity?

———

For each ecstatic instant
We must an anguish pay
In keen and quivering ratio
To the ecstasy.

For each beloved hour
Sharp pittances of years,
Bitter contested farthings
And coffers heaped with tears.

———

An altered look about the hills;
A Tyrian light the village fills;
A wider sunrise in the dawn;
A deeper twilight on the lawn;
A print of a vermilion foot;
A purple finger on the slope;
A flippant fly upon the pane;

A spider at his trade again;
An added strut in chanticleer;
A flower expected everywhere;
An axe shrill singing in the woods;
Fern-odors on untravelled roads,
All this, and more I cannot tell,
A furtive look you know as well,
And Nicodemus' mystery
Receives its annual reply.

———

Some, too fragile for winter winds,
The thoughtful grave encloses,—
Tenderly tucking them in from frost
Before their feet are cold.

Never the treasures in her nest
The cautious grave exposes,
Building where schoolboy dare not look
And sportsman is not bold.

This covert have all the children
Early aged, and often cold,—
Sparrows unnoticed by the Father;
Lambs for whom time had not a fold.

———

Delayed till she had ceased to know,
    Delayed till in its vest of snow
  Her loving bosom lay.
An hour behind the fleeting breath,
Later by just an hour than death,—
    Oh, lagging yesterday!

Could she have guessed that it would be;
Could but a crier of the glee
  Have climbed the distant hill;
Had not the bliss so slow a pace,—
Who knows but this surrendered face
  Were undefeated still?

Oh, if there may departing be
Any forgot by victory
  In her imperial round,
Show them this meek apparelled thing,
That could not stop to be a king,
  Doubtful if it be crowned!

———

Our lives are Swiss,—
  So still, so cool,
Till, some odd afternoon,
The Alps neglect their curtains,
  And we look farther on.

Italy stands the other side,
  While, like a guard between,
The solemn Alps,
The siren Alps,
  Forever intervene!

———

Some rainbow coming from the fair!
Some vision of the World Cashmere
I confidently see!
Or else a peacock's purple train,
Feather by feather, on the plain
Fritters itself away!

The dreamy butterflies bestir,
Lethargic pools resume the whir
Of last year's sundered tune.
From some old fortress on the sun
Baronial bees march, one by one,
In murmuring platoon!

The robins stand as thick to-day
As flakes of snow stood yesterday,
On fence and roof and twig.
The orchis binds her feather on
For her old lover, Don the Sun,
Revisiting the bog!

Without commander, countless, still,
The regiment of wood and hill
In bright detachment stand.
Behold! Whose multitudes are these?
The children of whose turbaned seas,
Or what Circassian land?

———

'Twas such a little, little boat
That toddled down the bay!
'Twas such a gallant, gallant sea
That beckoned it away!

'Twas such a greedy, greedy wave
That licked it from the coast;
Nor ever guessed the stately sails
My little craft was lost!

———

Going to heaven!
I don't know when,
Pray do not ask me how,—
Indeed, I'm too astonished
To think of answering you!
Going to heaven!—
How dim it sounds!
And yet it will be done
As sure as flocks go home at night
Unto the shepherd's arm!

Perhaps you're going too!
Who knows?
If you should get there first,
Save just a little place for me
Close to the two I lost!
The smallest "robe" will fit me,
And just a bit of "crown";
For you know we do not mind our dress
When we are going home.

I'm glad I don't believe it,
For it would stop my breath,
And I'd like to look a little more
At such a curious earth!
I am glad they did believe it
Whom I have never found
Since the mighty autumn afternoon
I left them in the ground.

———

Water is taught by thirst;
Land, by the oceans passed;
   Transport, by throe;
Peace, by its battles told;
Love, by memorial mould;
   Birds, by the snow.

———

Heart not so heavy as mine,
Wending late home,
As it passed my window
Whistled itself a tune,—

A careless snatch, a ballad,
A ditty of the street;
Yet to my irritated ear
An anodyne so sweet,

It was as if a bobolink,
Sauntering this way,
Carolled and mused and carolled,
Then bubbled slow away.

It was as if a chirping brook
Upon a toilsome way
Set bleeding feet to minuets
Without the knowing why.

To-morrow, night will come again,
Weary, perhaps, and sore.
Ah, bugle, by my window,
I pray you stroll once more!

———

The bee is not afraid of me,
I know the butterfly;
The pretty people in the woods
Receive me cordially.

The brooks laugh louder when I come,
The breezes madder play.
Wherefore, mine eyes, thy silver mists?
Wherefore, O summer's day?

———

I bring an unaccustomed wine
To lips long parching, next to mine,
And summon them to drink.

Crackling with fever, they essay;
I turn my brimming eyes away,
And come next hour to look.

The hands still hug the tardy glass;
The lips I would have cooled, alas!
Are so superfluous cold,

I would as soon attempt to warm
The bosoms where the frost has lain
Ages beneath the mould.

Some other thirsty there may be
To whom this would have pointed me
Had it remained to speak.

And so I always bear the cup
If, haply, mine may be the drop
Some pilgrim thirst to slake,—

If, haply, any say to me,
"Unto the little, unto me,"
When I at last awake.

———

Some things that fly there be,—
Birds, hours, the bumble-bee:
Of these no elegy.

Some things that stay there be,—
Grief, hills, eternity:
Nor this behooveth me.

There are, that resting, rise.
Can I expound the skies?
How still the riddle lies!

These are the days when birds come back,
A very few, a bird or two,
To take a backward look.

These are the days when skies put on
The old, old sophistries of June,—
A blue and gold mistake.

Oh, fraud that cannot cheat the bee,
Almost thy plausibility
Induces my belief,

Till ranks of seeds their witness bear,
And softly through the altered air
Hurries a timid leaf!

Oh, sacrament of summer days,
Oh, last communion in the haze,
Permit a child to join,

Thy sacred emblems to partake,
Thy consecrated bread to break,
Taste thine immortal wine!

Our share of night to bear,
Our share of morning,
Our blank in bliss to fill,
Our blank in scorning.

Here a star, and there a star,
Some lose their way.
Here a mist, and there a mist,
Afterwards—day!

———

Who never lost, are unprepared
A coronet to find;
Who never thirsted, flagons
And cooling tamarind.

Who never climbed the weary league—
Can such a foot explore
The purple territories
On Pizarro's shore?

How many legions overcome?
The emperor will say.
How many colors taken
On Revolution Day?

How many bullets bearest?
The royal scar hast thou?
Angels, write "Promoted"
On this soldier's brow!

———

I never hear the word "escape"
Without a quicker blood,
A sudden expectation,
A flying attitude.

I never hear of prisons broad
By soldiers battered down,
But I tug childish at my bars,—
Only to fail again!

———

Besides the autumn poets sing,
A few prosaic days
A little this side of the snow
And that side of the haze.

A few incisive mornings,
A few ascetic eves,—
Gone Mr. Bryant's golden rod,
And Mr. Thomson's sheaves.

Still is the bustle in the brook,
Sealed are the spicy valves;
Mesmeric fingers softly touch
The eyes of many elves

Perhaps a squirrel may remain,
My sentiments to share.
Grant me, O Lord, a sunny mind,
Thy windy will to bear!

———

Exultation is the going
Of an inland soul to sea,—
Past the houses, past the headlands,
Into deep eternity!

Bred as we, among the mountains,
Can the sailor understand
The divine intoxication
Of the first league out from land?

———

One dignity delays for all,
One mitred afternoon
None can avoid this purple,
None evade this crown.

Coach it insures, and footmen,
Chamber and state and throng;
Bells, also, in the village,
As we ride grand along.

What dignified attendants,
What service when we pause!
How loyally at parting
Their hundred hats they raise!

How pomp surpassing ermine,
When simple you and I
Present our meek escutcheon,
And claim the rank to die!

———

As children bid the guest good-night,
And then reluctant turn,
My flowers raise their pretty lips,
Then put their nightgowns on.

As children caper when they wake,
Merry that it is morn,
My flowers from a hundred cribs
Will peep, and prance again.

———

Will there really be a morning?
Is there such a thing as day?
Could I see it from the mountains
If I were as tall as they?

Has it feet like water-lilies?
Has it feathers like a bird?
Is it brought from famous countries
Of which I have never heard?

Oh, some scholar! Oh, some sailor!
Oh, some wise man from the skies!
Please to tell a little pilgrim
Where the place called morning lies!

———

Perhaps you'd like to buy a flower?
But I could never sell.
If you would like to borrow
Until the daffodil

Unties her yellow bonnet
Beneath the village door,
Until the bees, from clover rows
Their hock and sherry draw,

Why, I will lend until just then,
But not an hour more!

———

What inn is this
Where for the night
Peculiar traveller comes?
Who is the landlord?
Where the maids?
Behold, what curious rooms!
No ruddy fires on the hearth,
No brimming tankards flow.
Necromancer, landlord,
Who are these below?

———

Talk with prudence to a beggar
Of "Potosi" and the mines!
Reverently to the hungry
Of your viands and your wines!

Cautious, hint to any captive
You have passed enfranchised feet!
Anecdotes of air in dungeons
Have sometimes proved deadly sweet!

———

South winds jostle them.
Bumblebees come,
Hover, hesitate,
Drink, and are gone.

Butterflies pause
On their passage Cashmere;
I, softly plucking,
Present them here!

———

Went up a year this evening!
I recollect it well!
Amid no bells nor bravos
The bystanders will tell!
Cheerful, as to the village,
Tranquil, as to repose,
Chastened, as to the chapel,
This humble tourist rose.
Did not talk of returning,
Alluded to no time
When, were the gales propitious,
We might look for him;

Was grateful for the roses
In life's diverse bouquet,
Talked softly of new species
To pick another day.
Beguiling thus the wonder,
The wondrous nearer drew;
Hands bustled at the moorings—
The crowd respectful grew.
Ascended from our vision
To countenances new!
A difference, a daisy,
Is all the rest I knew!

———

New feet within my garden go,
New fingers stir the sod;
A troubadour upon the elm
Betrays the solitude.

New children play upon the green,
New weary sleep below;
And still the pensive spring returns,
And still the punctual snow!

———

So bashful when I spied her,
So pretty, so ashamed!
So hidden in her leaflets,
Lest anybody find;

So breathless till I passed her,
So helpless when I turned
And bore her, struggling, blushing,
Her simple haunts beyond!

For whom I robbed the dingle,
For whom betrayed the dell,
Many will doubtless ask me,
But I shall never tell!

———

Within my reach!
I could have touched!
I might have chanced that way!
Soft sauntered through the village
Sauntered as soft away!
So unsuspected violets
Within the fields lie low,
Too late for striving fingers
That passed, an hour ago.

———

"Whose are the little beds," I asked,
"Which in the valleys lie?"
Some shook their heads, and others smiled,
And no one made reply.

"Perhaps they did not hear," I said;
"I will inquire again.
Whose are the beds, the tiny beds
So thick upon the plain?"

" 'Tis daisy in the shortest;
A little farther on,
Nearest the door to wake the first,
Little leontodon.

" 'Tis iris, sir, and aster,
Anemone and bell,
Batschia in the blanket red,
And chubby daffodil."

Meanwhile at many cradles
Her busy foot she plied,
Humming the quaintest lullaby
That ever rocked a child.

"Hush! Epigea wakens!
The crocus stirs her lids,
Rhodora's cheek is crimson,—
She's dreaming of the woods."

Then, turning from them, reverent,
"Their bed time 'tis," she said;
"The bumble-bees will wake them
When April woods are red."

———

My nosegays are for captives;
    Dim, long-expectant eyes,
Fingers denied the plucking,
    Patient till paradise.

To such, if they should whisper
    Of morning and the moor,
They bear no other errand,
    And I, no other prayer.

———

Soul, wilt thou toss again?
By just such a hazard
Hundreds have lost, indeed,
But tens have won an all.

Angels' breathless ballot
Lingers to record thee;
Imps in eager caucus
Raffle for my soul.

———

Safe in their alabaster chambers,
Untouched by morning and untouched by noon,
Sleep the meek members of the resurrection,
Rafter of satin, and roof of stone.

Light laughs the breeze in her castle of sunshine;
Babbles the bee in a stolid ear;
Pipe the sweet birds in ignorant cadence,—
Ah, what sagacity perished here!

Grand go the years in the crescent above them;
Worlds scoop their arcs, and firmaments row,
Diadems drop and Doges surrender,
Soundless as dots on a disk of snow.

———

Except to heaven, she is nought;
Except for angels, lone;
Except to some wide-wandering bee,
A flower superfluous blown;

Except for winds, provincial;
Except by butterflies,
Unnoticed as a single dew
That on the acre lies.

The smallest housewife in the grass,
Yet take her from the lawn,
And somebody has lost the face
That made existence home!

———

The skies can't keep their secret!
They tell it to the hills—
The hills just tell the orchards—
And they the daffodils!

A bird, by chance, that goes that way
Soft overheard the whole.
If I should bribe the little bird,
Who knows but she would tell?

I think I won't, however,
It's finer not to know;
If summer were an axiom,
What sorcery had snow?

So keep your secret, Father!
I would not, if I could,
Know what the sapphire fellows do,
In your new-fashioned world!

————

Though I get home how late, how late!
So I get home, 'twill compensate.
Better will be the ecstasy
That they have done expecting me,
When, night descending, dumb and dark,
They hear my unexpected knock.
Transporting must the moment be,
Brewed from decades of agony!

To think just how the fire will burn,
Just how long-cheated eyes will turn
To wonder what myself will say,
And what itself will say to me,
Beguiles the centuries of way!

————

The murmur of a bee
A witchcraft yieldeth me.
If any ask me why,
'Twere easier to die
Than tell.

The red upon the hill
Taketh away my will;
If anybody sneer,
Take care, for God is here,
That's all.

The breaking of the day
Addeth to my degree;
If any ask me how,
Artist, who drew me so,
Must tell!

———

My river runs to thee:
Blue sea, wilt welcome me?

My river waits reply.
Oh sea, look graciously!

I'll fetch thee brooks
From spotted nooks,—

Say, sea,
Take me!

———

A wounded deer leaps highest,
I've heard the hunter tell;
'Tis but the ecstasy of death,
And then the brake is still.

The smitten rock that gushes,
The trampled steel that springs;
A cheek is always redder
Just where the hectic stings!

Mirth is the mail of anguish,
In which it cautious arm,
Lest anybody spy the blood
And "You're hurt" exclaim!

——

Come slowly, Eden!
Lips unused to thee,
Bashful, sip thy jasmines,
As the fainting bee,

Reaching late his flower,
Round her chamber hums,
Counts his nectars—enters,
And is lost in balms!

——

If I shouldn't be alive
When the robins come,
Give the one in red cravat
A memorial crumb.

If I couldn't thank you,
Being just asleep,
You will know I'm trying
With my granite lip!

——

I should not dare to leave my friend,
Because—because if he should die
While I was gone, and I—too late—
Should reach the heart that wanted me;

If I should disappoint the eyes
That hunted, hunted so, to see,
And could not bear to shut until
They "noticed" me—they noticed me;

If I should stab the patient faith
So sure I'd come—so sure I'd come,
It listening, listening, went to sleep
Telling my tardy name,—

My heart would wish it broke before,
Since breaking then, since breaking then,
Were useless as next morning's sun,
Where midnight frosts had lain!

———

As if some little Arctic flower,
Upon the polar hem,
Went wandering down the latitudes,
Until it puzzled came
To continents of summer,
To firmaments of sun,
To strange, bright crowds of flowers,
And birds of foreign tongue!
I say, as if this little flower
To Eden wandered in—
What then? Why, nothing, only
Your inference therefrom!

———

To learn the transport by the pain,
As blind men learn the sun;
To die of thirst, suspecting
That brooks in meadows run;

To stay the homesick, homesick feet
Upon a foreign shore
Haunted by native lands, the while,
And blue, beloved air—

This is the sovereign anguish,
This, the signal woe!
These are the patient laureates
Whose voices, trained below,

Ascend in ceaseless carol,
Inaudible, indeed,
To us, the duller scholars
Of the mysterious bard!

———

I'm wife; I've finished that,
That other state;
I'm Czar, I'm woman now:
It's safer so.

How odd the girl's life looks
Behind this soft eclipse!
I think that earth seems so
To those in heaven now.

This being comfort, then
That other kind was pain;
But why compare?
I'm wife! stop there!

———

Musicians wrestle everywhere:
All day, among the crowded air,
    I hear the silver strife;
And—waking long before the dawn—
Such transport breaks upon the town
    I think it that "new life"!

It is not bird, it has no nest;
Nor band, in brass and scarlet dressed,
   Nor tambourine, nor man;
It is not hymn from pulpit read,—
The morning stars the treble led
   On time's first afternoon!

Some say it is the spheres at play!
Some say that bright majority
   Of vanished dames and men!
Some think it service in the place
Where we, with late, celestial face,
   Please God, shall ascertain!

An awful tempest mashed the air,
The clouds were gaunt and few;
A black, as of a spectre's cloak,
Hid heaven and earth from view.

The creatures chuckled on the roofs
And whistled in the air,
And shook their fists and gnashed their teeth,
And swung their frenzied hair.

The morning lit, the birds arose;
The monster's faded eyes
Turned slowly to his native coast,
And peace was Paradise!

'Tis so much joy! 'Tis so much joy!
If I should fail, what poverty!
And yet, as poor as I
Have ventured all upon a throw;
Have gained! Yes! Hesitated so
This side the victory!

Life is but life, and death but death!
Bliss is but bliss, and breath but breath!
And if, indeed, I fail,
At least to know the worst is sweet.
Defeat means nothing but defeat,
No drearier can prevail!

And if I gain,—oh, gun at sea,
Oh, bells that in the steeples be,
At first repeat it slow!
For heaven is a different thing
Conjectured, and waked sudden in,
And might o'erwhelm me so!

———

I shall know why, when time is over,
And I have ceased to wonder why;
Christ will explain each separate anguish
In the fair schoolroom of the sky.

He will tell me what Peter promised,
And I, for wonder at his woe,
I shall forget the drop of anguish
That scalds me now, that scalds me now.

———

The rose did caper on her cheek,
Her bodice rose and fell,
Her pretty speech, like drunken men,
Did stagger pitiful.

Her fingers fumbled at her work,—
Her needle would not go;
What ailed so smart a little maid
It puzzled me to know,

Till opposite I spied a cheek
That bore another rose;
Just opposite, another speech
That like the drunkard goes;

A vest that, like the bodice, danced
To the immortal tune,—
Till those two troubled little clocks
Ticked softly into one.

———

On this long storm the rainbow rose,
On this late morn the sun;
The clouds, like listless elephants,
Horizons straggled down.

The birds rose smiling in their nests,
The gales indeed were done;
Alas! how heedless were the eyes
On whom the summer shone!

The quiet nonchalance of death
No daybreak can bestir;
The slow archangel's syllables
Must awaken her.

———

Wait till the majesty of Death
Invests so mean a brow!
Almost a powdered footman
Might dare to touch it now!

Wait till in everlasting robes
This democrat is dressed,
Then prate about "preferment"
And "station" and the rest!

Around this quiet courtier
Obsequious angels wait!
Full royal is his retinue,
Full purple is his state!

A lord might dare to lift the hat
To such a modest clay,
Since that my Lord, "the Lord of lords"
Receives unblushingly!

————

I lost a world the other day.
Has anybody found?
You'll know it by the row of stars
Around its forehead bound.

A rich man might not notice it;
Yet to my frugal eye
Of more esteem than ducats.
Oh, find it, sir, for me!

————

Just lost when I was saved!
Just felt the world go by!
Just girt me for the onset with eternity,
When breath blew back,
And on the other side
I heard recede the disappointed tide!

Therefore, as one returned, I feel,
Odd secrets of the line to tell!
Some sailor, skirting foreign shores,
Some pale reporter from the awful doors
Before the seal!

Next time, to stay!
Next time, the things to see
By ear unheard,
Unscrutinized by eye.

Next time, to tarry,
While the ages steal,—
Slow tramp the centuries,
And the cycles wheel.

———

At last to be identified!
At last, the lamps upon thy side,
The rest of life to see!
Past midnight, past the morning star!
Past sunrise! Ah! what leagues there are
Between our feet and day!

———

It's such a little thing to weep,
    So short a thing to sigh;
And yet by trades the size of these
    We men and women die!

———

How many times these low feet staggered,
Only the soldered mouth can tell;
Try! can you stir the awful rivet?
Try! can you lift the hasps of steel?

Stroke the cool forehead, hot so often,
Lift, if you can, the listless hair;
Handle the adamantine fingers
Never a thimble more shall wear.

Buzz the dull flies on the chamber window;
Brave shines the sun through the freckled pane;
Fearless the cobweb swings from the ceiling—
Indolent housewife, in daisies lain!

———

Two swimmers wrestled on the spar
Until the morning sun,
When one turned smiling to the land.
O God, the other one!

The stray ships passing spied a face
Upon the waters borne,
With eyes in death still begging raised,
And hands beseeching thrown.

———

I taste a liquor never brewed,
From tankards scooped in pearl;
Not all the vats upon the Rhine
Yield such an alcohol!

Inebriate of air am I,
And debauchee of dew,
Reeling, through endless summer days,
From inns of molten blue.

When landlords turn the drunken bee
Out of the foxglove's door,
When butterflies renounce their drams,
I shall but drink the more!

Till seraphs swing their snowy hats,
And saints to windows run,
To see the little tippler
Leaning against the sun!

———

The thought beneath so slight a film
Is more distinctly seen,—
As laces just reveal the surge,
Or mists the Apennine.

———

Portraits are to daily faces
As an evening west
To a fine, pedantic sunshine
In a satin vest.

———

I felt a funeral in my brain,
    And mourners, to and fro,
Kept treading, treading, till it seemed
    That sense was breaking through.

And when they all were seated,
    A service like a drum
Kept beating, beating, till I thought
    My mind was going numb.

And then I heard them lift a box,
   And creak across my soul
With those same boots of lead, again.
   Then space began to toll

As all the heavens were a bell,
  And Being but an ear,
And I and silence some strange race,
   Wrecked, solitary, here.

———

What if I say I shall not wait?
What if I burst the fleshly gate
And pass, escaped, to thee?
What if I file this mortal off,
See where it hurt me,—that's enough,—
And wade in liberty?

They cannot take us any more,—
Dungeons may call, and guns implore;
Unmeaning now, to me,
As laughter was an hour ago,
Or laces, or a travelling show,
Or who died yesterday!

———

The only ghost I ever saw
Was dressed in mechlin,—so;
He wore no sandal on his foot,
And stepped like flakes of snow.
His gait was soundless, like the bird,
But rapid, like the roe;
His fashions quaint, mosaic,
Or, haply, mistletoe.

His conversation seldom,
His laughter like the breeze
That dies away in dimples
Among the pensive trees.
Our interview was transient,—
Of me, himself was shy;
And God forbid I look behind
Since that appalling day!

There's a certain slant of light
On winter afternoons,
That oppresses, like the weight
Of cathedral tunes.

Heavenly hurt it gives us;
We can find no scar,
But internal difference
Where the meanings are.

None may teach it anything,
'Tis the seal, despair,—
An imperial affliction
Sent us of the air.

When it comes, the landscape listens,
Shadows hold their breath;
When it goes, 'tis like the distance
On the look of death.

How the old mountains drip with sunset,
   And the brake of dun!
How the hemlocks are tipped in tinsel
   By the wizard sun!

How the old steeples hand the scarlet,
    Till the ball is full,—
Have I the lip of the flamingo
    That I dare to tell?

Then, how the fire ebbs like billows,
    Touching all the grass
With a departing, sapphire feature,
    As if a duchess pass!

How a small dusk crawls on the village
    Till the houses blot;
And the odd flambeaux no men carry
    Glimmer on the spot!

Now it is night in nest and kennel,
    And where was the wood,
Just a dome of abyss is nodding
    Into solitude!—

These are the visions baffled Guido;
    Titian never told;
Domenichino dropped the pencil,
    Powerless to unfold.

I'm nobody! Who are you?
Are you nobody, too?
Then there's a pair of us—don't tell
They'd banish us, you know.

How dreary to be somebody!
How public, like a frog
To tell your name the livelong day
To an admiring bog!

I know some lonely houses off the road
A robber'd like the look of,—
Wooden barred,
And windows hanging low,
Inviting to
A portico,

Where two could creep:
One hand the tools,
The other peep
To make sure all's asleep.
Old-fashioned eyes,
Not easy to surprise!

How orderly the kitchen'd look by night,
With just a clock,—
But they could gag the tick,
And mice won't bark;
And so the walls don't tell,
None will.

A pair of spectacles ajar just stir—
An almanac's aware.
Was it the mat winked,
Or a nervous star?
The moon slides down the stair
To see who's there.

There's plunder,—where?
Tankard, or spoon,
Earring, or stone,
A watch, some ancient brooch
To match the grandmamma,
Staid sleeping there.

Day rattles, too,
Stealth's slow;
The sun has got as far
As the third sycamore.
Screams chanticleer,
"Who's there?"

And echoes, trains away,
Sneer—"Where?"
While the old couple, just astir,
Fancy the sunrise left the door ajar!

———

Wild nights! Wild nights!
Were I with thee,
Wild nights should be
Our luxury!

Futile the winds
To a heart in port,—
Done with the compass,
Done with the chart.

Rowing in Eden!
Ah! the sea!
Might I but moor
To-night in thee!

———

I think just how my shape will rise
When I shall be forgiven,
Till hair and eyes and timid head
Are out of sight, in heaven.

I think just how my lips will weigh
With shapeless, quivering prayer
That you, so late, consider me,
The sparrow of your care.

I mind me that of anguish sent,
Some drifts were moved away
Before my simple bosom broke,—
And why not this, if they?

And so, until delirious borne
I con that thing,—"forgiven,"—
Till with long fright and longer trust
I drop my heart, unshriven!

———

Heaven is what I cannot reach!
    The apple on the tree,
Provided it do hopeless hang,
    That "heaven" is, to me.

The color on the cruising cloud,
    The interdicted ground
Behind the hill, the house behind,—
    There Paradise is found!

———

This is the land the sunset washes,
These are the banks of the Yellow Sea;
Where it rose, or whither it rushes,
These are the western mystery!

Night after night her purple traffic
Strews the landing with opal bales;
Merchantmen poise upon horizons,
Dip, and vanish with fairy sails.

———

Blazing in gold and quenching in purple,
Leaping like leopards to the sky,
Then at the feet of the old horizon
Laying her spotted face, to die;

Stooping as low as the otter's window,
Touching the roof and tinting the barn,
Kissing her bonnet to the meadow,—
And the juggler of day is gone!

———

Hope is the thing with feathers
That perches in the soul,
And sings the tune without the words
And never stops at all,

And sweetest in the gale is heard;
And sore must be the storm
That could abash the little bird
That kept so many warm.

I've heard it in the chillest land,
And on the strangest sea;
Yet, never, in extremity,
It asked a crumb of me.

———

Father, I bring thee not myself,—
    That were the little load;
I bring thee the imperial heart
    I had not strength to hold.

The heart I cherished in my own
    Till mine too heavy grew,
Yet strangest, heavier since it went,
    Is it too large for you?

———

It can't be summer,—that got through;
It's early yet for spring;
There's that long town of white to cross
Before the blackbirds sing.

It can't be dying,—it's too rouge,—
The dead shall go in white.
So sunset shuts my question down
With clasps of chrysolite.

———

She sweeps with many-colored brooms,
And leaves the shreds behind;
Oh, housewife in the evening west,
Come back, and dust the pond!

You dropped a purple ravelling in,
You dropped an amber thread;
And now you've littered all the East
With duds of emerald!

And still she plies her spotted brooms,
And still the aprons fly,
Till brooms fade softly into stars—
And then I come away.

———

A solemn thing it was, I said,
   A woman white to be,
And wear, if God should count me fit
   Her hallowed mystery.

A timid thing to drop a life
   Into the purple well,
Too plummetless that it come back
   Eternity until.

———

I like a look of agony,
Because I know it's true;
Men do not sham convulsion,
Nor simulate a throe.

The eyes glaze once, and that is death.
Impossible to feign
The beads upon the forehead
By homely anguish strung.

———

Doubt me, my dim companion!
Why, God would be content
With but a fraction of the love
Poured thee without a stint.
The whole of me, forever,
What more the woman can,—
Say quick, that I may dower thee
With last delight I own!

It cannot be my spirit,
For that was thine before;
I ceded all of dust I knew,—
What opulence the more
Had I, a humble maiden,
Whose farthest of degree
Was that she might
Some distant heaven,
Dwell timidly with thee!

———

Tie the strings to my life, my Lord,
    Then I am ready to go!
Just a look at the horses—
    Rapid! That will do!

Put me in on the firmest side,
　So I shall never fall;
For we must ride to the Judgment,
　And it's partly down hill.

But never I mind the bridges,
　And never I mind the sea;
Held fast in everlasting race
　By my own choice and thee.

Good-by to the life I used to live,
　And the world I used to know;
And kiss the hills for me, just once;
　Now I am ready to go!

———

I breathed enough to learn the trick,
　And now, removed from air,
I simulate the breath so well,
　That one, to be quite sure

The lungs are stirless, must descend
　Among the cunning cells,
And touch the pantomime himself.
　How cool the bellows feels!

———

A clock stopped—not the mantel's;
　Geneva's farthest skill
Can't put the puppet bowing
　That just now dangled still.

An awe came on the trinket!
　The figures hunched with pain,
Then quivered out of decimals
　Into degreeless noon.

It will not stir for doctors,
    This pendulum of snow;
The shopman importunes it,
    While cool, concernless No

Nods from the gilded pointers,
    Nods from the seconds slim,
Decades of arrogance between
    The dial life and him.

———

I held a jewel in my fingers
And went to sleep.
The day was warm, and winds were prosy
I said: " 'Twill keep."

I woke and chid my honest fingers,—
The gem was gone;
And now an amethyst remembrance
Is all I own.

———

The sun just touched the morning;
The morning, happy thing,
Supposed that he had come to dwell,
And life would be all spring.

She felt herself supremer,—
A raised, ethereal thing;
Henceforth for her what holiday!
Meanwhile, her wheeling king

Trailed slow along the orchards
His haughty, spangled hems,
Leaving a new necessity,—
The want of diadems!

The morning fluttered, staggered,
Felt feebly for her crown,—
Her unanointed forehead
Henceforth her only one.

———

I can wade grief,
Whole pools of it,—
I'm used to that.
But the least push of joy
Breaks up my feet,
And I tip—drunken.
Let no pebble smile,
'Twas the new liquor,—
That was all!

Power is only pain,
Stranded, through discipline,
Till weights will hang.
Give balm to giants,
And they'll wilt, like men.
Give Himmaleh,—
They'll carry him!

———

Of bronze and blaze
    The north, to-night!
  So adequate its forms,
So preconcerted with itself,
    So distant to alarms,—
An unconcern so sovereign
    To universe, or me,
It paints my simple spirit
    With tints of majesty,
Till I take vaster attitudes,
    And strut upon my stem,
Disdaining men and oxygen,
    For arrogance of them.

My splendors are menagerie;
   But their completeless show
Will entertain the centuries
   When I am, long ago,
An island in dishonored grass,
   Whom none but daisies know.

———

Good night! which put the candle out?
A jealous zephyr, not a doubt.
   Ah! friend, you little knew
How long at that celestial wick
The angels labored diligent;
   Extinguished, now, for you!

It might have been the lighthouse spark
Some sailor, rowing in the dark,
   Had importuned to see!
It might have been the waning lamp
That lit the drummer from the camp
   To purer reveille!

———

He put the belt around my life,—
I heard the buckle snap,
And turned away, imperial,
My lifetime folding up
Deliberate, as a duke would do
A kingdom's title-deed,—
Henceforth a dedicated sort,
A member of the cloud.

Yet not too far to come at call,
And do the little toils
That make the circuit of the rest,
And deal occasional smiles
To lives that stoop to notice mine
And kindly ask it in,—
Whose invitation, knew you not
For whom I must decline?

———

A shady friend for torrid days
Is easier to find
Than one of higher temperature
For frigid hour of mind.

The vane a little to the east
Scares muslin souls away;
If broadcloth breasts are firmer
Than those of organdy,

Who is to blame? The weaver?
Ah! the bewildering thread!
The tapestries of paradise
So notelessly are made!

———

If I may have it when it's dead
    I will contented be;
If just as soon as breath is out
    It shall belong to me,

Until they lock it in the grave,
    'Tis bliss I cannot weigh,
For though they lock thee in the grave,
    Myself can hold the key.

Think of it, lover! I and thee
    Permitted face to face to be;
After a life, a death we'll say,—
    For death was that, and this is thee.

———

Delight becomes pictorial
When viewed through pain,—
More fair, because impossible
That any gain.

The mountain at a given distance
In amber lies;
Approached, the amber flits a little,—
And that's the skies!

———

I found the phrase to every thought
I ever had, but one;
And that defies me,—as a hand
Did try to chalk the sun

To races nurtured in the dark;—
How would your own begin?
Can blaze be done in cochineal,
Or noon in mazarin?

———

The body grows outside,—
The more convenient way,—
That if the spirit like to hide,
Its temple stands alway

Ajar, secure, inviting;
It never did betray
The soul that asked its shelter
In timid honesty.

———

Like mighty footlights burned the red
At bases of the trees,—
The far theatricals of day
Exhibiting to these.

'Twas universe that did applaud
While, chiefest of the crowd,
Enabled by his royal dress,
Myself distinguished God.

———

A toad can die of light!
    Death is the common right
 Of toads and men,—
Of earl and midge
The privilege.
    Why swagger then?
The gnat's supremacy
Is large as thine.

———

I had been hungry all the years;
My noon had come, to dine;
I, trembling, drew the table near,
And touched the curious wine.

'Twas this on tables I had seen,
When turning, hungry, lone,
I looked in windows, for the wealth
I could not hope to own.

I did not know the ample bread,
'Twas so unlike the crumb
The birds and I had often shared
In Nature's dining-room.

The plenty hurt me, 'twas so new,—
Myself felt ill and odd,
As berry of a mountain bush
Transplanted to the road.

Nor was I hungry; so I found
That hunger was a way
Of persons outside windows,
The entering takes away.

———

Pain has an element of blank;
It cannot recollect
When it began, or if there were
A day when it was not.

It has no future but itself,
Its infinite realms contain
Its past, enlightened to perceive
New periods of pain.

———

I gave myself to him,
And took himself for pay.
The solemn contract of a life
Was ratified this way.

The wealth might disappoint,
Myself a poorer prove
Than this great purchaser suspect,
The daily own of Love

Depreciates the vision;
But, till the merchant buy,
Still fable, in the isles of spice,
The subtle cargoes lie.

At least, 'tis mutual risk,—
Some found it mutual gain;
Sweet debt of Life,—each night to owe,
Insolvent, every noon.

———

I like to see it lap the miles,
And lick the valleys up,
And stop to feed itself at tanks;
And then, prodigious, step

Around a pile of mountains,
And, supercilious, peer
In shanties by the sides of roads;
And then a quarry pare

To fit its sides, and crawl between,
Complaining all the while
In horrid, hooting stanza;
Then chase itself down hill

And neigh like Boanerges;
Then, punctual as a star,
Stop—docile and omnipotent—
At its own stable door.

———

The night was wide, and furnished scant
With but a single star,
That often as a cloud it met
Blew out itself for fear.

The wind pursued the little bush,
And drove away the leaves
November left; then clambered up
And fretted in the eaves.

No squirrel went abroad;
A dog's belated feet
Like intermittent plush were heard
Adown the empty street.

To feel if blinds be fast,
And closer to the fire
Her little rocking-chair to draw,
And shiver for the poor,

The housewife's gentle task.
"How pleasanter," said she
Unto the sofa opposite,
"The sleet than May—no thee!"

———

Afraid? Of whom am I afraid?
Not death; for who is he?
The porter of my father's lodge
As much abasheth me.

Of life? 'Twere odd I fear a thing
That comprehendeth me
In one or more existences
At Deity's decree.

Of resurrection? Is the east
Afraid to trust the morn
With her fastidious forehead?
As soon impeach my crown!

———

Unto my books so good to turn
Far ends of tired days;
It half endears the abstinence,
And pain is missed in praise.

As flavors cheer retarded guests
With banquetings to be,
So spices stimulate the time
Till my small library.

It may be wilderness without,
Far feet of failing men,
But holiday excludes the night,
And it is bells within.

I thank these kinsmen of the shelf;
Their countenances bland
Enamour in prospective,
And satisfy, obtained.

———

When I was small, a woman died.
To-day her only boy
Went up from the Potomac,
His face all victory,

To look at her, how slowly
The seasons must have turned
Till bullets clipt an angle,
And he passed quickly round!

If pride shall be in Paradise
I never can decide;
Of their imperial conduct,
No person testified.

But proud in apparition,
That woman and her boy
Pass back and forth before my brain,
As ever in the sky.

———

Glee! the great storm is over!
Four have recovered the land;
Forty gone down together
Into the boiling sand.

Ring, for the scant salvation!
Toll, for the bonnie souls,—
Neighbor and friend and bridegroom,
Spinning upon the shoals!

How they will tell the shipwreck
When winter shakes the door,
Till the children ask, "But the forty?
Did they come back no more?"

Then a silence suffuses the story,
And a softness the teller's eye;
And the children no further question,
And only the waves reply.

———

Our journey had advanced;
Our feet were almost come
To that odd fork in Being's road,
Eternity by term.

Our pace took sudden awe,
Our feet reluctant led.
Before were cities, but between,
The forest of the dead.

Retreat was out of hope,—
Behind, a sealèd route,
Eternity's white flag before,
And God at every gate.

———

'Twas a long parting, but the time
For interview had come;
Before the judgment-seat of God,
The last and second time

These fleshless lovers met,
A heaven in a gaze,
A heaven of heavens, the privilege
Of one another's eyes.

No lifetime set on them,
Apparelled as the new
Unborn, except they had beheld,
Born everlasting now.

Was bridal e'er like this?
A paradise, the host,
And cherubim and seraphim
The most familiar guest.

———

It makes no difference abroad,
The seasons fit the same,
The mornings blossom into noons,
And split their pods of flame.

Wild-flowers kindle in the woods,
The brooks brag all the day;
No blackbird bates his jargoning
For passing Calvary.

Auto-da-fé and judgment
Are nothing to the bee;
His separation from his rose
To him seems misery.

———

To know just how he suffered would be dear;
To know if any human eyes were near
To whom he could intrust his wavering gaze,
Until it settled firm on Paradise.

To know if he was patient, part content,
Was dying as he thought, or different;
Was it a pleasant day to die,
And did the sunshine face his way?

What was his furthest mind, of home, or God,
Or what the distant say
At news that he ceased human nature
On such a day?

And wishes, had he any?
Just his sigh, accented,
Had been legible to me.
And was he confident until
Ill fluttered out in everlasting well?

And if he spoke, what name was best,
What first,
What one broke off with
At the drowsiest?

Was he afraid, or tranquil?
Might he know
How conscious consciousness could grow,
Till love that was, and love too blest to be,
Meet—and the junction be Eternity?

———

I asked no other thing,
No other was denied.
I offered Being for it;
The mighty merchant smiled.

Brazil? He twirled a button.
Without a glance my way:
"But, madam, is there nothing else
That we can show to-day?"

———

I years had been from home,
And now, before the door,
I dared not open, lest a face
I never saw before

Stare vacant into mine
And ask my business there.
My business,—just a life I left,
Was such still dwelling there?

I fumbled at my nerve,
I scanned the windows near;
The silence like an ocean rolled,
And broke against my ear.

I laughed a wooden laugh
That I could fear a door,
Who danger and the dead had faced,
But never quaked before.

I fitted to the latch
My hand, with trembling care,
Lest back the awful door should spring,
And leave me standing there.

I moved my fingers off
As cautiously as glass,
And held my ears, and like a thief
Fled gasping from the house.

———

It was too late for man,
But early yet for God;
Creation impotent to help,
But prayer remained our side.

How excellent the heaven,
When earth cannot be had;
How hospitable, then, the face
Of our old neighbor, God!

———

The way I read a letter's this:
'Tis first I lock the door,
And push it with my fingers next,
For transport it be sure.

And then I go the furthest off
To counteract a knock;
Then draw my little letter forth
And softly pick its lock.

Then, glancing narrow at the wall,
And narrow at the floor,
For firm conviction of a mouse
Not exorcised before,

Peruse how infinite I am
To—no one that you know!
And sigh for lack of heaven,—but not
The heaven the creeds bestow.

———

The brain is wider than the sky,
    For, put them side by side,
The one the other will include
    With ease, and you beside.

The brain is deeper than the sea,
    For, hold them, blue to blue,
The one the other will absorb,
    As sponges, buckets do.

The brain is just the weight of God,
    For, lift them, pound for pound,
And they will differ, if they do,
    As syllable from sound.

———

I cannot live with you,
It would be life,
And life is over there
Behind the shelf

The sexton keeps the key to,
Putting up
Our life, his porcelain,
Like a cup

Discarded of the housewife,
Quaint or broken;
A newer Sèvres pleases,
Old ones crack.

I could not die with you,
For one must wait
To shut the other's gaze down,—
You could not.

And I, could I stand by
And see you freeze,
Without my right of frost,
Death's privilege?

Nor could I rise with you,
Because your face
Would put out Jesus',
That new grace

Glow plain and foreign
On my homesick eye,
Except that you, than he
Shone closer by.

They'd judge us—how?
For you served Heaven, you know,
Or sought to;
I could not,

Because you saturated sight,
And I had no more eyes
For sordid excellence
As Paradise.

And were you lost, I would be,
Though my name
Rang loudest
On the heavenly fame.

And were you saved,
And I condemned to be
Where you were not,
That self were hell to me.

So we must keep apart,
You there, I here,
With just the door ajar
That oceans are,
And prayer,
And that pale sustenance,
Despair!

———

Could I but ride indefinite,
  As doth the meadow-bee,
And visit only where I liked,
  And no man visit me,

And flirt all day with buttercups,
  And marry whom I may,
And dwell a little everywhere,
  Or better, run away

With no police to follow,
  Or chase me if I do,
Till I should jump peninsulas
  To get away from you,—

I said, but just to be a bee
  Upon a raft of air,
And row in nowhere all day long,
  And anchor off the bar,—
What liberty! So captives deem
  Who tight in dungeons are.

———

A little road not made of man,
Enabled of the eye,
Accessible to thill of bee,
Or cart of butterfly.

If town it have, beyond itself,
'Tis that I cannot say;
I only sigh,—no vehicle
Bears me along that way.

———

Of all the souls that stand create
I have elected one.
When sense from spirit flies away,
And subterfuge is done;

When that which is and that which was
Apart, intrinsic, stand,
And this brief tragedy of flesh
Is shifted like a sand;

When figures show their royal front
And mists are carved away,—
Behold the atom I preferred
To all the lists of clay!

———

You left me, sweet, two legacies,—
A legacy of love
A Heavenly Father would content,
Had He the offer of;

You left me boundaries of pain
Capacious as the sea,
Between eternity and time,
Your consciousness and me.

———

A long, long sleep, a famous sleep
  That makes no show for dawn
By stretch of limb or stir of lid,—
  An independent one.

Was ever idleness like this?
  Within a hut of stone
To bask the centuries away
  Nor once look up for noon?

———

The soul unto itself
Is an imperial friend,—
Or the most agonizing spy
An enemy could send.

Secure against its own,
No treason it can fear;
Itself its sovereign, of itself
The soul should stand in awe.

———

This is my letter to the world,
  That never wrote to me,—
The simple news that Nature told,
  With tender majesty.

Her message is committed
  To hands I cannot see;
For love of her, sweet countrymen,
  Judge tenderly of me!

———

It sifts from leaden sieves,
It powders all the wood,
It fills with alabaster wool
The wrinkles of the road.

It makes an even face
Of mountain and of plain,—
Unbroken forehead from the east
Unto the east again.

It reaches to the fence,
It wraps it, rail by rail,
Till it is lost in fleeces;
It flings a crystal veil

On stump and stack and stem,—
The summer's empty room,
Acres of seams where harvests were,
Recordless, but for them.

It ruffles wrists of posts,
As ankles of a queen,—
Then stills its artisans like ghosts,
Denying they have been.

———

A bird came down the walk:
He did not know I saw;
He bit an angle-worm in halves
And ate the fellow, raw.

And then he drank a dew
From a convenient grass,
And then hopped sidewise to the wall
To let a beetle pass.

He glanced with rapid eyes
That hurried all abroad,—
They looked like frightened beads, I thought
He stirred his velvet head

Like one in danger; cautious,
I offered him a crumb,
And he unrolled his feathers
And rowed him softer home

Than oars divide the ocean,
Too silver for a seam,
Or butterflies, off banks of noon,
Leap, plashless, as they swim.

———

The nearest dream recedes, unrealized.
      The heaven we chase
      Like the June bee
      Before the school-boy
      Invites the race,
      Stoops to an easy clover—
Dips—evades—teases—deploys;
      Then to the royal clouds
      Lifts his light pinnace
      Heedless of the boy
Staring, bewildered, at the mocking sky.

      Homesick for steadfast honey,
         Ah! the bee flies not
That brews that rare variety.

———

I'll tell you how the sun rose,—
A ribbon at a time.
The steeples swam in amethyst,
The news like squirrels ran.

The hills untied their bonnets,
The bobolinks begun.
Then I said softly to myself,
"That must have been the sun!"

.   .   .   .   .

But how he set, I know not.
There seemed a purple stile
Which little yellow boys and girls
Were climbing all the while

Till when they reached the other side,
A dominie in gray
Put gently up the evening bars,
And led the flock away.

————

The day came slow, till five o'clock,
Then sprang before the hills
Like hindered rubies, or the light
A sudden musket spills.

The purple could not keep the east,
The sunrise shook from fold,
Like breadths of topaz, packed a night,
The lady just unrolled.

The happy winds their timbrels took;
The birds, in docile rows,
Arranged themselves around their prince—
(The wind is prince of those).

The orchard sparkled like a jewel,—
How mighty 'twas, to stay
A guest in this stupendous place,
The parlor of the day!

————

The soul selects her own society,
Then shuts the door;
On her divine majority
Obtrude no more.

Unmoved, she notes the chariot's pausing
At her low gate;
Unmoved, an emperor is kneeling
Upon her mat.

I've known her from an ample nation
Choose one;
Then close the valves of her attention
Like stone.

———

I reason, earth is short,
And anguish absolute,
And many hurt;
But what of that?

I reason, we could die:
The best vitality
Cannot excel decay;
But what of that?

I reason that in heaven
Somehow, it will be even,
Some new equation given;
But what of that?

———

The one that could repeat the summer day
Were greater than itself, though he
Minutest of mankind might be.
And who could reproduce the sun,
At period of going down—
The lingering and the stain, I mean—
When Orient has been outgrown,
And Occident becomes unknown,
His name remain.

———

Of all the sounds despatched abroad,
There's not a charge to me
Like that old measure in the boughs,
That phraseless melody

The wind does, working like a hand
Whose fingers brush the sky,
Then quiver down, with tufts of tune
Permitted gods and me.

When winds go round and round in bands,
And thrum upon the door,
And birds take places overhead,
To bear them orchestra,

I crave him grace of summer boughs,
If such an outcast be,
He never heard that fleshless chant
Rise solemn in the tree,

As if some caravan of sound
On deserts, in the sky,
Had broken rank,
Then knit, and passed
In seamless company.

———

I should have been too glad, I see,
Too lifted for the scant degree
    Of life's penurious round;
My little circuit would have shamed
This new circumference, have blamed
    The homelier time behind.

I should have been too saved, I see,
Too rescued; fear too dim to me
    That I could spell the prayer
I knew so perfect yesterday,—
That scalding one, "Sabachthani,"
    Recited fluent here.

Earth would have been too much, I see,
And heaven not enough for me;
    I should have had the joy
Without the fear to justify,—
The palm without the Calvary;
    So, Saviour, crucify.

Defeat whets victory, they say;
The reefs in old Gethsemane
    Endear the shore beyond.
'Tis beggars banquets best define;
'Tis thirsting vitalizes wine,—
    Faith faints to understand.

————

We play at paste,
Till qualified for pearl,
Then drop the paste,
And deem ourself a fool.
The shapes, though, were similar,
And our new hands
Learned gem-tactics
Practising sands.

————

Before I got my eye put out,
I liked as well to see
As other creatures that have eyes,
And know no other way.

But were it told to me, to-day,
That I might have the sky
For mine, I tell you that my heart
Would split, for size of me.

The meadows mine, the mountains mine,—
All forests, stintless stars,
As much of noon as I could take
Between my finite eyes.

The motions of the dipping birds,
The lightning's jointed road,
For mine to look at when I liked,—
The news would strike me dead!

So, safer, guess, with just my soul
Upon the window-pane
Where other creatures put their eyes,
Incautious of the sun.

———

Some keep the Sabbath going to church;
I keep it staying at home,
With a bobolink for a chorister,
And an orchard for a dome.

Some keep the Sabbath in surplice;
I just wear my wings,
And instead of tolling the bell for church,
Our little sexton sings.

God preaches,—a noted clergyman,—
And the sermon is never long;
So instead of getting to heaven at last,
I'm going all along!

———

Your riches taught me poverty.
Myself a millionaire
In little wealths,—as girls could boast,—
Till broad as Buenos Ayre,

You drifted your dominions
A different Peru;
And I esteemed all poverty,
For life's estate with you.

Of mines I little know, myself,
But just the names of gems,—
The colors of the commonest;
And scarce of diadems

So much that, did I meet the queen,
Her glory I should know:
But this must be a different wealth,
To miss it beggars so.

I'm sure 'tis India all day
To those who look on you
Without a stint, without a blame,—
Might I but be the Jew!

I'm sure it is Golconda,
Beyond my power to deem,—
To have a smile for mine each day,
How better than a gem!

At least, it solaces to know
That there exists a gold,
Although I prove it just in time
Its distance to behold!

It's far, far treasure to surmise,
And estimate the pearl
That slipped my simple fingers through
While just a girl at school!

———

There came a day at summer's full
Entirely for me;
I thought that such were for the saints,
Where revelations be.

The sun, as common, went abroad,
The flowers, accustomed, blew,
As if no soul the solstice passed
That maketh all things new.

The time was scarce profaned by speech;
The symbol of a word
Was needless, as at sacrament
The wardrobe of our Lord.

Each was to each the sealèd church,
Permitted to commune this time,
Lest we too awkward show
At supper of the Lamb.

The hours slid fast, as hours will,
Clutched tight by greedy hands;
So faces on two decks look back,
Bound to opposing lands.

And so, when all the time had failed,
Without external sound,
Each bound the other's crucifix,
We gave no other bond.

Sufficient troth that we shall rise—
Deposed, at length, the grave—
To that new marriage, justified
Through Calvaries of Love!

————

I know a place where summer strives
With such a practised frost,
She each year leads her daisies back,
Recording briefly, "Lost."

But when the south wind stirs the pools
And struggles in the lanes,
Her heart misgives her for her vow,
And she pours soft refrains

Into the lap of adamant,
And spices, and the dew,
That stiffens quietly to quartz,
Upon her amber shoe.

————

A murmur in the trees to note,
  Not loud enough for wind;
A star not far enough to seek,
  Nor near enough to find;

A long, long yellow on the lawn,
  A hubbub as of feet;
Not audible, as ours to us,
  But dapperer, more sweet;

A hurrying home of little men
    To houses unperceived,—
All this, and more, if I should tell,
    Would never be believed.

Of robins in the trundle bed
    How many I espy
Whose nightgowns could not hide the wings,
    Although I heard them try!

But then I promised ne'er to tell;
    How could I break my word?
So go your way and I'll go mine,
    No fear you'll miss the road.

———

There's been a death in the opposite house
    As lately as to-day,
I know it by the numb look
    Such houses have alway.

The neighbors rustle in and out,
    The doctor drives away.
A window opens like a pod,
    Abrupt, mechanically;

Somebody flings a mattress out,—
    The children hurry by;
They wonder if It died on that,—
    I used to when a boy.

The minister goes stiffly in
    As if the house were his,
And he owned all the mourners now,
    And little boys besides;

And then the milliner, and the man
  Of the appalling trade,
To take the measure of the house.
  There'll be that dark parade

Of tassels and of coaches soon;
  It's easy as a sign,—
The intuition of the news
  In just a country town.

———

A charm invests a face
Imperfectly beheld,—
The lady dare not lift her veil
For fear it be dispelled.

But peers beyond her mesh,
And wishes, and denies,—
Lest interview annul a want
That image satisfies.

———

No rack can torture me,
My soul's at liberty.
Behind this mortal bone
There knits a bolder one

You cannot prick with saw,
Nor rend with scimitar.
Two bodies therefore be;
Bind one, and one will flee.

The eagle of his nest
No easier divest
And gain the sky,
Than mayest thou,

Except thyself may be
Thine enemy;
Captivity is consciousness,
So's liberty.

———

It struck me every day
   The lightning was as new
As if the cloud that instant slit
   And let the fire through.

It burned me in the night,
   It blistered in my dream;
It sickened fresh upon my sight
   With every morning's beam.

I thought that storm was brief,—
   The maddest, quickest by;
But Nature lost the date of this,
   And left it in the sky.

———

Death sets a thing significant
The eye had hurried by,
Except a perished creature
Entreat us tenderly

To ponder little workmanships
In crayon or in wool,
With "This was last her fingers did,"
Industrious until

The thimble weighed too heavy,
The stitches stopped themselves,
And then 'twas put among the dust
Upon the closet shelves.

A book I have, a friend gave,
Whose pencil, here and there,
Had notched the place that pleased him,—
At rest his fingers are.

Now, when I read, I read not,
For interrupting tears
Obliterate the etchings
Too costly for repairs.

————

When night is almost done,
And sunrise grows so near
That we can touch the spaces,
It's time to smooth the hair

And get the dimples ready,
And wonder we could care
For that old faded midnight
That frightened but an hour.

————

I went to heaven,—
'Twas a small town,
Lit with a ruby,
Lathed with down.
Stiller than the fields
At the full dew,
Beautiful as pictures
No man drew.
People like the moth,
Of mechlin frames,
Duties of gossamer,
And eider names.

Almost contented
I could be
'Mong such unique
Society.

———

I read my sentence steadily,
Reviewed it with my eyes,
To see that I made no mistake
In its extremest clause,—

The date, and manner of the shame;
And then the pious form
That "God have mercy" on the soul
The jury voted him.

I made my soul familiar
With her extremity,
That at the last it should not be
A novel agony,

But she and Death, acquainted,
Meet tranquilly as friends,
Salute and pass without a hint—
And there the matter ends.

———

He fumbles at your spirit
    As players at the keys
Before they drop full music on;
    He stuns you by degrees.

Prepares your brittle substance
    For the ethereal blow,
By fainter hammers, further heard,
    Then nearer, then so slow

Your breath has time to straighten,
   Your brain to bubble cool,—
Deals one imperial thunderbolt
   That scalps your naked soul.

———

The moon is distant from the sea,
And yet with amber hands
She leads him, docile as a boy,
Along appointed sands.

He never misses a degree;
Obedient to her eye,
He comes just so far toward the town,
Just so far goes away.

Oh, Signor, thine the amber hand,
And mine the distant sea,—
Obedient to the last command
Thine eyes impose on me.

———

There is a flower that bees prefer,
And butterflies desire;
To gain the purple democrat
The humming-birds aspire.

And whatsoever insect pass,
A honey bears away
Proportioned to his several dearth
And her capacity.

Her face is rounder than the moon,
And ruddier than the gown
Of orchis in the pasture,
Or rhododendron worn.

She doth not wait for June;
Before the world is green
Her sturdy little countenance
Against the wind is seen,

Contending with the grass,
Near kinsman to herself,
For privilege of sod and sun,
Sweet litigants for life.

And when the hills are full,
And newer fashions blow,
Doth not retract a single spice
For pang of jealousy.

Her public is the noon,
Her providence the sun,
Her progress by the bee proclaimed
In sovereign, swerveless tune.

The bravest of the host,
Surrendering the last,
Nor even of defeat aware
When cancelled by the frost.

———

I gained it so,
By climbing slow,
By catching at the twigs that grow
Between the bliss and me.
It hung so high,
As well the sky
Attempt by strategy.

I said I gained it,—
    This was all.
Look, how I clutch it,
    Lest it fall,
And I a pauper go;
Unfitted by an instant's grace
For the contented beggar's face
I wore an hour ago.

———

Dare you see a soul at the white heat?
    Then crouch within the door.
Red is the fire's common tint;
    But when the vivid ore

Has sated flame's conditions,
    Its quivering substance plays
Without a color but the light
    Of unanointed blaze.

Least village boasts its blacksmith,
    Whose anvil's even din
Stands symbol for the finer forge
    That soundless tugs within,

Refining these impatient ores
    With hammer and with blaze,
Until the designated light
    Repudiate the forge.

———

From cocoon forth a butterfly
As lady from her door
Emerged—a summer afternoon—
Repairing everywhere,

Without design, that I could trace,
Except to stray abroad
On miscellaneous enterprise
The clovers understood.

Her pretty parasol was seen
Contracting in a field
Where men made hay, then struggling hard
With an opposing cloud,

Where parties, phantom as herself,
To Nowhere seemed to go
In purposeless circumference,
As 'twere a tropic show.

And notwithstanding bee that worked,
And flower that zealous blew,
This audience of idleness
Disdained them, from the sky,

Till sundown crept, a steady tide,
And men that made the hay,
And afternoon, and butterfly,
Extinguished in its sea.

———

Prayer is the little implement
Through which men reach
Where presence is denied them.
They fling their speech

By means of it in God's ear;
If then He hear,
This sums the apparatus
Comprised in prayer.

———

Much madness is divinest sense
To a discerning eye;
Much sense the starkest madness.
'Tis the majority
In this, as all, prevails.
Assent, and you are sane;
Demur,—you're straightway dangerous,
And handled with a chain.

———

The wind tapped like a tired man,
And like a host, "Come in,"
I boldly answered; entered then
My residence within

A rapid, footless guest,
To offer whom a chair
Were as impossible as hand
A sofa to the air.

No bone had he to bind him,
His speech was like the push
Of numerous humming-birds at once
From a superior bush.

His countenance a billow,
His fingers, if he pass,
Let go a music, as of tunes
Blown tremulous in glass.

He visited, still flitting;
Then, like a timid man,
Again he tapped—'twas flurriedly—
And I became alone.

———

A precious, mouldering pleasure 'tis
To meet an antique book,
In just the dress his century wore;
A privilege, I think,

His venerable hand to take,
And warming in our own,
A passage back, or two, to make
To times when he was young.

His quaint opinions to inspect,
His knowledge to unfold
On what concerns our mutual mind,
The literature of old;

What interested scholars most,
What competitions ran
When Plato was a certainty,
And Sophocles a man;

When Sappho was a living girl,
And Beatrice wore
The gown that Dante deified.
Facts, centuries before,

He traverses familiar,
As one should come to town
And tell you all your dreams were true:
He lived where dreams were sown.

His presence is enchantment,
You beg him not to go;
Old volumes shake their vellum heads
And tantalize, just so.

———

I dreaded that first robin so,
But he is mastered now,
And I'm accustomed to him grown,—
He hurts a little, though.

I thought if I could only live
Till that first shout got by,
Not all pianos in the woods
Had power to mangle me.

I dared not meet the daffodils,
For fear their yellow gown
Would pierce me with a fashion
So foreign to my own.

I wished the grass would hurry,
So when 'twas time to see,
He'd be too tall, the tallest one
Could stretch to look at me.

I could not bear the bees should come,
I wished they'd stay away
In those dim countries where they go:
What word had they for me?

They're here, though; not a creature failed,
No blossom stayed away
In gentle deference to me,
The Queen of Calvary.

Each one salutes me as he goes,
And I my childish plumes
Lift, in bereaved acknowledgment
Of their unthinking drums.

———

What soft, cherubic creatures
　　These gentlewomen are!
One would as soon assault a plush
　　Or violate a star.

Such dimity convictions,
　　A horror so refined
Of freckled human nature,
　　Of Deity ashamed,—

It's such a common glory,
　　A fisherman's degree!
Redemption, brittle lady,
　　Be so ashamed of thee.

———

They dropped like flakes, they dropped like stars,
　　Like petals from a rose,
When suddenly across the June
　　A wind with fingers goes.

They perished in the seamless grass,—
　　No eye could find the place;
But God on his repealless list
　　Can summon every face.

———

I went to thank her,
But she slept;
Her bed a funnelled stone,
With nosegays at the head and foot,
That travellers had thrown,

Who went to thank her;
But she slept.
'Twas short to cross the sea
To look upon her like, alive,
But turning back 'twas slow.

———

Me! Come! My dazzled face
In such a shining place!

Me! Hear! My foreign ear
The sounds of welcome near!

The saints shall meet
Our bashful feet.

My holiday shall be
That they remember me;

My paradise, the fame
That they pronounce my name.

———

To lose one's faith surpasses
   The loss of an estate,
Because estates can be
   Replenished,—faith cannot.

Inherited with life,
   Belief but once can be;
Annihilate a single clause,
   And Being's beggary.

———

I know that he exists
Somewhere, in silence.
He has hid his rare life
From our gross eyes.

'Tis in instant's play,
'Tis a fond ambush,
Just to make bliss
Earn her own surprise!

But should the play
Prove piercing earnest,
Should the glee glaze
In death's stiff stare,

Would not the fun
Look too expensive?
Would not the jest
Have crawled too far?

———

God made a little gentian;
It tried to be a rose
And failed, and all the summer laughed.
But just before the snows
There came a purple creature
That ravished all the hill;
And summer hid her forehead,
And mockery was still.
The frosts were her condition;
The Tyrian would not come
Until the North evoked it.
"Creator! shall I bloom?"

———

Two butterflies went out at noon
And waltzed above a stream,
Then stepped straight through the firmament
And rested on a beam;

And then together bore away
Upon a shining sea,—
Though never yet, in any port,
Their coming mentioned be.

If spoken by the distant bird,
If met in ether sea
By frigate or by merchantman,
Report was not to me.

———

'Twas just this time last year I died.
    I know I heard the corn,
When I was carried by the farms,—
    It had the tassels on.

I thought how yellow it would look
    When Richard went to mill;
And then I wanted to get out,
    But something held my will.

I thought just how red apples wedged
    The stubble's joints between;
And carts went stooping round the fields
    To take the pumpkins in.

I wondered which would miss me least,
    And when Thanksgiving came,
If father'd multiply the plates
    To make an even sum.

And if my stocking hung too high,
    Would it blur the Christmas glee,
That not a Santa Claus could reach
    The altitude of me?

But this sort grieved myself, and so
   I thought how it would be
When just this time, some perfect year,
   Themselves should come to me.

———

Of tribulation these are they
Denoted by the white;
The spangled gowns, a lesser rank
Of victors designate.

All these did conquer; but the ones
Who overcame most times
Wear nothing commoner than snow,
No ornament but palms.

Surrender is a sort unknown
On this superior soil;
Defeat, an outgrown anguish,
Remembered as the mile

Our panting ankle barely gained
When night devoured the road;
But we stood whispering in the house,
And all we said was "Saved!"

———

I died for beauty, but was scarce
Adjusted in the tomb,
When one who died for truth was lain
In an adjoining room.

He questioned softly why I failed?
"For beauty," I replied.
"And I for truth,—the two are one;
We brethren are," he said.

And so, as kinsmen met a night,
We talked between the rooms,
Until the moss had reached our lips,
And covered up our names.

———

If anybody's friend be dead,
It's sharpest of the theme
The thinking how they walked alive,
At such and such a time.

Their costume, of a Sunday,
Some manner of the hair,—
A prank nobody knew but them,
Lost, in the sepulchre.

How warm they were on such a day:
You almost feel the date,
So short way off it seems; and now,
They're centuries from that.

How pleased they were at what you said;
You try to touch the smile,
And dip your fingers in the frost:
When was it, can you tell,

You asked the company to tea,
Acquaintance, just a few,
And chatted close with this grand thing
That don't remember you?

Past bows and invitations,
Past interview, and vow,
Past what ourselves can estimate,—
That makes the quick of woe!

———

The grass so little has to do,—
A sphere of simple green,
With only butterflies to brood,
And bees to entertain,

And stir all day to pretty tunes
The breezes fetch along,
And hold the sunshine in its lap
And bow to everything;

And thread the dews all night, like pearls,
And make itself so fine,—
A duchess were too common
For such a noticing.

And even when it dies, to pass
In odors so divine,
As lowly spices gone to sleep,
Or amulets of pine.

And then to dwell in sovereign barns,
And dream the days away,—
The grass so little has to do,
I wish I were the hay!

———

The brain within its groove
Runs evenly and true;
But let a splinter swerve,
'Twere easier for you
To put the water back
When floods have slit the hills,
And scooped a turnpike for themselves,
And blotted out the mills!

———

I heard a fly buzz when I died;
  The stillness round my form
Was like the stillness in the air
  Between the heaves of storm.

The eyes beside had wrung them dry,
  And breaths were gathering sure
For that last onset, when the king
  Be witnessed in his power.

I willed my keepsakes, signed away
  What portion of me I
Could make assignable,—and then
  There interposed a fly,

With blue, uncertain, stumbling buzz,
  Between the light and me;
And then the windows failed, and then
  I could not see to see.

———

He touched me, so I live to know
  That such a day, permitted so,
I groped upon his breast.
It was a boundless place to me,
And silenced, as the awful sea
  Puts minor streams to rest.

And now, I'm different from before,
As if I breathed superior air,
  Or brushed a royal gown;
My feet, too, that had wandered so,
My gypsy face transfigured now
  To tenderer renown.

———

It was not death, for I stood up,
And all the dead lie down;
It was not night, for all the bells
Put out their tongues, for noon.

It was not frost, for on my flesh
I felt siroccos crawl,—
Nor fire, for just my marble feet
Could keep a chancel cool.

And yet it tasted like them all;
The figures I have seen
Set orderly, for burial,
Reminded me of mine,

As if my life were shaven
And fitted to a frame,
And could not breathe without a key;
And 'twas like midnight, some,

When everything that ticked has stopped,
And space stares, all around,
Or grisly frosts, first autumn morns,
Repeal the beating ground.

But most like chaos,—stopless, cool,—
Without a chance or spar,
Or even a report of land
To justify despair.

———

We cover thee, sweet face.
   Not that we tire of thee,
But that thyself fatigue of us;
   Remember, as thou flee,
We follow thee until
   Thou notice us no more,

And then, reluctant, turn away
    To con thee o'er and o'er,
And blame the scanty love
    We were content to show,
Augmented, sweet, a hundred fold
    If thou would'st take it now.

———

I took my power in my hand
And went against the world;
'Twas not so much as David had,
But I was twice as bold.

I aimed my pebble, but myself
Was all the one that fell.
Was it Goliath was too large,
Or only I too small?

———

Mine by the right of the white election!
Mine by the royal seal!
Mine by the sign in the scarlet prison
Bars cannot conceal!

Mine, here in vision and in veto!
Mine, by the grave's repeal
Titled, confirmed,—delirious charter!
Mine, while the ages steal!

———

Except the heaven had come so near,
So seemed to choose my door,
The distance would not haunt me so;
I had not hoped before.

But just to hear the grace depart
I never thought to see,
Afflicts me with a double loss;
'Tis lost, and lost to me.

———

Departed to the judgment,
A mighty afternoon;
Great clouds like ushers leaning,
Creation looking on.

The flesh surrendered, cancelled,
The bodiless begun;
Two worlds, like audiences, disperse
And leave the soul alone.

———

This world is not conclusion;
  A sequel stands beyond,
Invisible, as music,
  But positive, as sound.
It beckons and it baffles;
  Philosophies don't know,
And through a riddle, at the last,
  Sagacity must go.
To guess it puzzles scholars;
  To gain it, men have shown
Contempt of generations,
  And crucifixion known.

———

As far from pity as complaint,
  As cool to speech as stone,
As numb to revelation
  As if my trade were bone.

As far from time as history,
  As near yourself to-day
As children to the rainbow's scarf,
  Or sunset's yellow play

To eyelids in the sepulchre.
  How still the dancer lies,
While color's revelations break,
  And blaze the butterflies!

———

I measure every grief I meet
  With analytic eyes;
I wonder if it weighs like mine,
  Or has an easier size.

I wonder if they bore it long,
  Or did it just begin?
I could not tell the date of mine,
  It feels so old a pain.

I wonder if it hurts to live,
  And if they have to try,
And whether, could they choose between,
  They would not rather die.

I wonder if when years have piled—
  Some thousands—on the cause
Of early hurt, if such a lapse
  Could give them any pause;

Or would they go on aching still
  Through centuries above,
Enlightened to a larger pain
  By contrast with the love.

The grieved are many, I am told;
  The reason deeper lies,—
Death is but one and comes but once,
  And only nails the eyes.

There's grief of want, and grief of cold,—
    A sort they call "despair";
There's banishment from native eyes,
    In sight of native air.

And though I may not guess the kind
    Correctly, yet to me
A piercing comfort it affords
    In passing Calvary,

To note the fashions of the cross,
    Of those that stand alone,
Still fascinated to presume
    That some are like my own.

———

To hear an oriole sing
May be a common thing,
Or only a divine.

It is not of the bird
Who sings the same, unheard,
As unto crowd.

The fashion of the ear
Attireth that it hear
In dun or fair.

So whether it be rune,
Or whether it be none,
Is of within;

The "tune is in the tree,"
The sceptic showeth me;
"No, sir! In thee!"

———

At least to pray is left, is left.
O Jesus! in the air
I know not which thy chamber is,—
I'm knocking everywhere.

Thou stirrest earthquake in the South,
And maelstrom in the sea;
Say, Jesus Christ of Nazareth,
Hast thou no arm for me?

———

I had no cause to be awake,
My best was gone to sleep,
And morn a new politeness took
And failed to wake them up,

But called the others clear,
And passed their curtains by.
Sweet morning, when I over-sleep,
Knock, recollect, for me!

I looked at sunrise once,
And then I looked at them,
And wishfulness in me arose
For circumstance the same.

'Twas such an ample peace,
It could not hold a sigh,—
'Twas Sabbath with the bells divorced,
'Twas sunset all the day.

So choosing but a gown
And taking but a prayer,
The only raiment I should need,
I struggled, and was there.

———

'Tis little I could care for pearls
    Who own the ample sea;
Or brooches, when the Emperor
    With rubies pelteth me;

Or gold, who am the Prince of Mines;
    Or diamonds, when I see
A diadem to fit a dome
    Continual crowning me.

———

I started early, took my dog,
And visited the sea;
The mermaids in the basement
Came out to look at me,

And frigates in the upper floor
Extended hempen hands,
Presuming me to be a mouse
Aground, upon the sands.

But no man moved me till the tide
Went past my simple shoe,
And past my apron and my belt,
And past my bodice too,

And made as he would eat me up
As wholly as a dew
Upon a dandelion's sleeve—
And then I started too.

And he—he followed close behind;
I felt his silver heel
Upon my ankle,—then my shoes
Would overflow with pearl.

Until we met the solid town,
No man he seemed to know;
And bowing with a mighty look
At me, the sea withdrew.

———

I meant to have but modest needs,
Such as content, and heaven;
Within my income these could lie,
And life and I keep even.

But since the last included both,
It would suffice my prayer
But just for one to stipulate,
And grace would grant the pair.

And so, upon this wise I prayed,—
Great Spirit, give to me
A heaven not so large as yours,
But large enough for me.

A smile suffused Jehovah's face;
The cherubim withdrew;
Grave saints stole out to look at me,
And showed their dimples, too.

I left the place with all my might,—
My prayer away I threw;
The quiet ages picked it up,
And Judgment twinkled, too,

That one so honest be extant
As take the tale for true
That "Whatsoever you shall ask,
Itself be given you."

But I, grown shrewder, scan the skies
With a suspicious air,—
As children, swindled for the first,
All swindlers be, infer.

———

Triumph may be of several kinds.
There's triumph in the room
When that old imperator, Death,
By faith is overcome.

There's triumph of the finer mind
When truth, affronted long,
Advances calm to her supreme,
Her God her only throng.

A triumph when temptation's bribe
Is slowly handed back,
One eye upon the heaven renounced
And one upon the rack.

Severer triumph, by himself
Experienced, who can pass
Acquitted from that naked bar,
Jehovah's countenance!

———

I've seen a dying eye
Run round and round a room
In search of something, as it seemed,
Then cloudier become;
And then, obscure with fog,
And then be soldered down,
Without disclosing what it be,
'Twere blessed to have seen.

———

If you were coming in the fall,
I'd brush the summer by
With half a smile and half a spurn,
As housewives do a fly.

If I could see you in a year,
I'd wind the months in balls,
And put them each in separate drawers,
Until their time befalls.

If only centuries delayed,
I'd count them on my hand,
Subtracting till my fingers dropped
Into Van Diemen's land.

If certain, when this life was out,
That yours and mine should be,
I'd toss it yonder like a rind,
And taste eternity.

But now, all ignorant of the length
Of time's uncertain wing,
It goads me, like the goblin bee,
That will not state its sting.

———

That I did always love,
I bring thee proof:
That till I loved
I did not love enough.

That I shall love alway,
I offer thee
That love is life,
And life hath immortality.

This, dost thou doubt, sweet?
Then have I
Nothing to show
But Calvary.

———

I envy seas whereon he rides,
  I envy spokes of wheels
Of chariots that him convey,
  I envy speechless hills

That gaze upon his journey;
  How easy all can see
What is forbidden utterly
  As heaven, unto me!

I envy nests of sparrows
  That dot his distant eaves,
The wealthy fly upon his pane,
  The happy, happy leaves

That just abroad his window
  Have summer's leave to be,
The earrings of Pizarro
  Could not obtain for me.

I envy light that wakes him,
  And bells that boldly ring
To tell him it is noon abroad,—
  Myself his noon could bring,

Yet interdict my blossom
  And abrogate my bee,
Lest noon in everlasting night
  Drop Gabriel and me.

———

The heart asks pleasure first,
And then, excuse from pain;
And then, those little anodynes
That deaden suffering;

And then, to go to sleep;
And then, if it should be
The will of its Inquisitor,
The liberty to die.

———

"Going to him! Happy letter! Tell him—
Tell him the page I didn't write;
Tell him I only said the syntax,
And left the verb and the pronoun out.
Tell him just how the fingers hurried,
Then how they waded, slow, slow, slow;
And then you wished you had eyes in your pages,
So you could see what moved them so.

"Tell him it wasn't a practised writer,
You guessed, from the way the sentence toiled;
You could hear the bodice tug, behind you,
As if it held but the might of a child;
You almost pitied it, you, it worked so.
Tell him— No, you may quibble there,
For it would split his heart to know it,
And then you and I were silenter.

"Tell him night finished before we finished,
And the old clock kept neighing 'day!'
And you got sleepy and begged to be ended—
What could it hinder so, to say?
Tell him just how she sealed you, cautious,
But if he ask where you are hid
Until to-morrow,—happy letter!
Gesture, coquette, and shake your head!"

———

I had no time to hate, because
The grave would hinder me,
And life was not so ample I
Could finish enmity.

Nor had I time to love; but since
Some industry must be,
The little toil of love, I thought,
Was large enough for me.

———

I'm ceded, I've stopped being theirs;
The name they dropped upon my face
With water, in the country church,
Is finished using now,
And they can put it with my dolls,
My childhood, and the string of spools
I've finished threading too.

Baptized before without the choice,
But this time consciously, of grace
Unto supremest name,
Called to my full, the crescent dropped,
Existence's whole arc filled up
With one small diadem.

My second rank, too small the first,
Crowned, crowing on my father's breast,
A half unconscious queen;
But this time, adequate, erect,
With will to choose or to reject,
And I choose—just a throne.

———

I live with him, I see his face;
   I go no more away
For visitor, or sundown;
   Death's single privacy,

The only one forestalling mine,
    And that by right that he
Presents a claim invisible,
    No wedlock granted me.

I live with him, I hear his voice,
    I stand alive to-day
To witness to the certainty
    Of immortality

Taught me by Time,—the lower way,
    Conviction every day,—
That life like this is endless,
    Be judgment what it may.

———

I think the hemlock likes to stand
Upon a marge of snow;
It suits his own austerity,
And satisfies an awe

That men must slake in wilderness,
Or in the desert cloy,—
An instinct for the hoar, the bald,
Lapland's necessity.

The hemlock's nature thrives on cold;
The gnash of northern winds
Is sweetest nutriment to him,
His best Norwegian wines.

To satin races he is nought;
But children on the Don
Beneath his tabernacles play,
And Dnieper wrestlers run.

———

Through the straight pass of suffering
The martyrs even trod,
Their feet upon temptation,
Their faces upon God.

A stately, shriven company;
Convulsion playing round,
Harmless as streaks of meteor
Upon a planet's bound.

Their faith the everlasting troth;
Their expectation fair;
The needle to the north degree
Wades so, through polar air.

———

I meant to find her when I came;
    Death had the same design;
But the success was his, it seems,
    And the discomfit mine.

I meant to tell her how I longed
    For just this single time;
But Death had told her so the first,
    And she had hearkened him.

To wander now is my abode;
    To rest,—to rest would be
A privilege of hurricane
    To memory and me.

———

Their height in heaven comforts not,
Their glory nought to me;
'Twas best imperfect, as it was;
I'm finite, I can't see.

The house of supposition,
The glimmering frontier
That skirts the acres of perhaps,
To me shows insecure.

The wealth I had contented me;
If 'twas a meaner size,
Then I had counted it until
It pleased my narrow eyes

Better than larger values,
However true their show;
This timid life of evidence
Keeps pleading, "I don't know."

———

I lived on dread; to those who know
The stimulus there is
In danger, other impetus
Is numb and vital-less.

As 'twere a spur upon the soul,
A fear will urge it where
To go without the spectre's aid
Were challenging despair.

———

Remorse is memory awake,
Her companies astir,—
A presence of departed acts
At window and at door.

Its past set down before the soul,
And lighted with a match,
Perusal to facilitate
Of its condensed despatch.

Remorse is cureless,—the disease
Not even God can heal;
For 'tis His institution,—
The complement of hell.

———

Bereaved of all, I went abroad,
    No less bereaved to be
Upon a new peninsula,—
    The grave preceded me,

Obtained my lodgings ere myself,
    And when I sought my bed,
The grave it was, reposed upon
    The pillow for my head.

I waked, to find it first awake,
    I rose,—it followed me;
I tried to drop it in the crowd,
    To lose it in the sea,

In cups of artificial drowse
    To sleep its shape away,—
The grave was finished, but the spade
    Remained in memory.

———

One need not be a chamber to be haunted,
One need not be a house;
The brain has corridors surpassing
Material place.

Far safer, of a midnight meeting
External ghost,
Than an interior confronting
That whiter host.

Far safer through an Abbey gallop,
The stones achase,
Than, moonless, one's own self encounter
In lonesome place.

Ourself, behind ourself concealed,
Should startle most;
Assassin, hid in our apartment,
Be horror's least.

The prudent carries a revolver,
He bolts the door,
O'erlooking a superior spectre
More near.

———

Essential oils are wrung:
The attar from the rose
Is not expressed by suns alone,
It is the gift of screws.

The general rose decays;
But this, in lady's drawer,
Makes summer when the lady lies
In ceaseless rosemary.

———

It dropped so low in my regard
   I heard it hit the ground,
And go to pieces on the stones
   At bottom of my mind;

Yet blamed the fate that fractured, less
   Than I reviled myself
For entertaining plated wares
   Upon my silver shelf.

———

God gave a loaf to every bird,
But just a crumb to me;
I dare not eat it, though I starve,—
My poignant luxury
To own it, touch it, prove the feat
That made the pellet mine,—
Too happy in my sparrow chance
For ampler coveting.

It might be famine all around,
I could not miss an ear,
Such plenty smiles upon my board,
My garner shows so fair.
I wonder how the rich may feel,—
An Indiaman—an Earl?
I deem that I with but a crumb
Am sovereign of them all.

———

Because I could not stop for Death,
He kindly stopped for me;
The carriage held but just ourselves
And Immortality.

We slowly drove, he knew no haste,
And I had put away
My labor, and my leisure too,
For his civility.

We passed the school where children played
Their lessons scarcely done;
We passed the fields of gazing grain,
We passed the setting sun.

We paused before a house that seemed
A swelling of the ground;
The roof was scarcely visible,
The cornice but a mound.

Since then 'tis centuries; but each
Feels shorter than the day
I first surmised the horses' heads
Were toward eternity.

—

On the bleakness of my lot
   Bloom I strove to raise.
Late, my acre of a rock
   Yielded grape and maize.

Soil of flint if steadfast tilled
   Will reward the hand;
Seed of palm by Lybian sun
   Fructified in sand.

—

She rose to his requirement, dropped
The playthings of her life
To take the honorable work
Of woman and of wife.

If aught she missed in her new day
Of amplitude, or awe,
Or first prospective, or the gold
In using wore away,

It lay unmentioned, as the sea
Develops pearl and weed,
But only to himself is known
The fathoms they abide.

—

It tossed and tossed,—
A little brig I knew,—
O'ertook by blast,
It spun and spun,
And groped delirious, for morn.

It slipped and slipped,
As one that drunken stepped;
Its white foot tripped,
Then dropped from sight.

Ah, brig, good-night
To crew and you;
The ocean's heart too smooth, too blue,
To break for you.

———

You've seen balloons set, haven't you?
    So stately they ascend
It is as swans discarded you
    For duties diamond.

Their liquid feet go softly out
    Upon a sea of blond;
They spurn the air as 'twere too mean
    For creatures so renowned.

Their ribbons just beyond the eye,
    They struggle some for breath,
And yet the crowd applauds below;
    They would not encore death.

The gilded creature strains and spins,
    Trips frantic in a tree,
Tears open her imperial veins
    And tumbles in the sea.

The crowd retire with an oath,
    The dust in streets goes down,
And clerks in counting-rooms observe,
    " 'Twas only a balloon."

———

I many times thought peace had come,
When peace was far away;
As wrecked men deem they sight the land
At centre of the sea,

And struggle slacker, but to prove,
As hopelessly as I,
How many the fictitious shores
Before the harbor lie.

———

My worthiness is all my doubt,
    His merit all my fear,
Contrasting which, my qualities
    Do lowlier appear;

Lest I should insufficient prove
    For his beloved need,
The chiefest apprehension
    Within my loving creed.

So I, the undivine abode
    Of his elect content,
Conform my soul as 'twere a church
    Unto her sacrament.

———

A drop fell on the apple tree,
Another on the roof;
A half a dozen kissed the eaves,
And made the gables laugh.

A few went out to help the brook,
That went to help the sea.
Myself conjectured, Were they pearls,
What necklaces could be!

The dust replaced in hoisted roads,
The birds jocoser sung;
The sunshine threw his hat away,
The orchards spangles hung.

The breezes brought dejected lutes,
And bathed them in the glee;
The East put out a single flag,
And signed the fête away.

———

The sun kept setting, setting still;
No hue of afternoon
Upon the village I perceived,—
From house to house 'twas noon.

The dusk kept dropping, dropping still;
No dew upon the grass,
But only on my forehead stopped,
And wandered in my face.

My feet kept drowsing, drowsing still,
My fingers were awake;
Yet why so little sound myself
Unto my seeming make?

How well I knew the light before!
I could not see it now.
'Tis dying, I am doing; but
I'm not afraid to know.

————

We thirst at first,—'tis Nature's act;
    And later, when we die,
A little water supplicate
    Of fingers going by.

It intimates the finer want,
    Whose adequate supply
Is that great water in the west
    Termed immortality.

————

Victory comes late,
And is held low to freezing lips
Too rapt with frost
To take it.

How sweet it would have tasted,
Just a drop!
Was God so economical?
His table's spread too high for us
Unless we dine on tip-toe.
Crumbs fit such little mouths,
Cherries suit robins;
The eagle's golden breakfast
Strangles them.
God keeps his oath to sparrows,
Who of little love
Know how to starve!

————

Presentiment is that long shadow on the lawn
Indicative that suns go down;
The notice to the startled grass
That darkness is about to pass.

The moon was but a chin of gold
   A night or two ago,
And now she turns her perfect face
   Upon the world below.

Her forehead is of amplest blond;
   Her cheek like beryl stone;
Her eye unto the summer dew
   The likest I have known.

Her lips of amber never part;
   But what must be the smile
Upon her friend she could bestow
   Were such her silver will!

And what a privilege to be
   But the remotest star!
For certainly her way might pass
   Beside your twinkling door.

Her bonnet is the firmament,
   The universe her shoe,
The stars the trinkets at her belt,
   Her dimities of blue.

They say that "time assuages,"—
   Time never did assuage;
An actual suffering strengthens,
   As sinews do, with age.

Time is a test of trouble,
    But not a remedy.
If such it prove, it prove too
    There was no malady.

———

Each life converges to some centre
Expressed or still;
Exists in every human nature
A goal,

Admitted scarcely to itself, it may be,
Too fair
For credibility's temerity
To dare.

Adored with caution, as a brittle heaven,
To reach
Were hopeless as the rainbow's raiment
To touch,

Yet persevered toward, surer for the distance;
How high
Unto the saints' slow diligence
The sky!

Ungained, it may be, by life's low venture,
But then,
Eternity enables the endeavoring
Again.

———

Life, and Death, and Giants
    Such as these, are still.
Minor apparatus, hopper of the mill,
Beetle at the candle,
    Or a fife's small fame,
Maintain by accident
    That they proclaim.

———

Her final summer was it,
And yet we guessed it not;
If tenderer industriousness
Pervaded her, we thought

A further force of life
Developed from within,—
When Death lit all the shortness up,
And made the hurry plain.

We wondered at our blindness,—
When nothing was to see
But her Carrara guide-post,—
At our stupidity,

When, duller than our dulness,
The busy darling lay,
So busy was she, finishing,
So leisurely were we!

———

Alter? When the hills do.
Falter? When the sun
Question if his glory
Be the perfect one.

Surfeit? When the daffodil
Doth of the dew:
Even as herself, O friend!
I will of you!

———

Nature, the gentlest mother,
Impatient of no child,
The feeblest or the waywardest,—
Her admonition mild

In forest and the hill
By traveller is heard,
Restraining rampant squirrel
Or too impetuous bird.

How fair her conversation,
A summer afternoon,—
Her household, her assembly;
And when the sun goes down

Her voice among the aisles
Incites the timid prayer
Of the minutest cricket,
The most unworthy flower.

When all the children sleep
She turns as long away
As will suffice to light her lamps;
Then, bending from the sky,

With infinite affection
And infiniter care,
Her golden finger on her lip,
Wills silence everywhere.

———

A thought went up my mind to-day
That I have had before,
But did not finish,—some way back,
I could not fix the year,

Nor where it went, nor why it came
The second time to me,
Nor definitely what it was,
Have I the art to say.

But somewhere in my soul, I know
I've met the thing before;
It just reminded me—'twas all—
And came my way no more.

———

One blessing had I, than the rest
   So larger to my eyes
That I stopped gauging, satisfied,
   For this enchanted size.

It was the limit of my dream,
   The focus of my prayer,—
A perfect, paralyzing bliss
   Contented as despair.

I knew no more of want or cold,
   Phantasms both become,
For this new value in the soul,
   Supremest earthly sum.

The heaven below the heaven above
   Obscured with ruddier hue.
Life's latitude leant over-full;
   The judgment perished, too.

Why joys so scantily disburse,
   Why Paradise defer,
Why floods are served to us in bowls,—
   I speculate no more.

———

Like trains of cars on tracks of plush
I hear the level bee:
A jar across the flowers goes,
Their velvet masonry

Withstands until the sweet assault
Their chivalry consumes,
While he, victorious, tilts away
To vanquish other blooms.

His feet are shod with gauze,
His helmet is of gold;
His breast, a single onyx
With chrysoprase, inlaid.

His labor is a chant,
His idleness a tune;
Oh, for a bee's experience
Of clovers and of noon!

———

The robin is the one
That interrupts the morn
With hurried, few, express reports
When March is scarcely on.

The robin is the one
That overflows the noon
With her cherubic quantity,
An April but begun.

The robin is the one
That speechless from her nest
Submits that home and certainty
And sanctity are best.

———

Love is anterior to life,
    Posterior to death,
Initial of creation, and
    The exponent of breath.

———

I sing to use the waiting,
    My bonnet but to tie,
And shut the door unto my house;
    No more to do have I,

Till, his best step approaching,
    We journey to the day,
And tell each other how we sang
    To keep the dark away.

———

To my quick ear the leaves conferred;
    The bushes they were bells;
I could not find a privacy
    From Nature's sentinels.

In cave if I presumed to hide,
    The walls began to tell;
Creation seemed a mighty crack
    To make me visible.

———

The wind begun to rock the grass
With threatening tunes and low,—
He flung a menace at the earth,
A menace at the sky.

The leaves unhooked themselves from trees
And started all abroad;
The dust did scoop itself like hands
And throw away the road.

The wagons quickened on the streets,
The thunder hurried slow;
The lightning showed a yellow beak,
And then a livid claw.

The birds put up the bars to nests,
The cattle fled to barns;
There came one drop of giant rain,
And then, as if the hands

That held the dams had parted hold,
The waters wrecked the sky,
But overlooked my father's house,
Just quartering a tree.

———

If I can stop one heart from breaking,
I shall not live in vain;
If I can ease one life the aching,
Or cool one pain,
Or help one fainting robin
Unto his nest again,
I shall not live in vain.

———

It is an honorable thought,
    And makes one lift one's hat,
As one encountered gentlefolk
    Upon a daily street,

That we've immortal place,
   Though pyramids decay,
And kingdoms, like the orchard,
   Flit russetly away.

The mountain sat upon the plain
In his eternal chair,
His observation omnifold,
His inquest everywhere.

The seasons prayed around his knees,
Like children round a sire:
Grandfather of the days is he,
Of dawn the ancestor.

We outgrow love like other things
   And put it in the drawer,
Till it an antique fashion shows
   Like costumes grandsires wore.

Death is a dialogue between
The spirit and the dust.
"Dissolve," says Death. The Spirit, "Sir,
I have another trust."

Death doubts it, argues from the ground.
The Spirit turns away,
Just laying off, for evidence,
An overcoat of clay.

I stepped from plank to plank
  So slow and cautiously;
The stars about my head I felt,
  About my feet the sea.

I knew not but the next
  Would be my final inch,—
This gave me that precarious gait
  Some call experience.

———

A door just opened on a street—
  I, lost, was passing by—
An instant's width of warmth disclosed,
  And wealth, and company.

The door as sudden shut, and I,
  I, lost, was passing by,—
Lost doubly, but by contrast most,
  Enlightening misery.

———

Ample make this bed.
Make this bed with awe;
In it wait till judgment break
Excellent and fair.

Be its mattress straight,
Be its pillow round;
Let no sunrise' yellow noise
Interrupt this ground.

———

From us she wandered now a year,
  Her tarrying unknown;
If wilderness prevent her feet,
  Or that ethereal zone

No eye hath seen and lived,
    We ignorant must be.
We only know what time of year
    We took the mystery.

———

An everywhere of silver,
With ropes of sand
To keep it from effacing
The track called land.

———

This merit hath the worst,—
It cannot be again.
When Fate hath taunted last
And thrown her furthest stone,

The maimed may pause and breathe,
And glance securely round.
The deer invites no longer
Than it eludes the hound.

———

I felt a cleavage in my mind
    As if my brain had split;
I tried to match it, seam by seam,
    But could not make them fit.

The thought behind I strove to join
    Unto the thought before,
But sequence ravelled out of reach
    Like balls upon a floor.

———

A light exists in spring
   Not present on the year
At any other period.
   When March is scarcely here

A color stands abroad
   On solitary hills
That science cannot overtake,
   But human nature *feels*.

It waits upon the lawn;
   It shows the furthest tree
Upon the furthest slope we know;
   It almost speaks to me.

Then, as horizons step,
   Or noons report away,
Without the formula of sound,
   It passes, and we stay:

A quality of loss
   Affecting our content,
As trade had suddenly encroached
   Upon a sacrament.

———

A death-blow is a life-blow to some
Who, till they died, did not alive become;
Who, had they lived, had died, but when
They died, vitality begun.

———

I never saw a moor,
I never saw the sea;
Yet know I how the heather looks,
And what a wave must be.

I never spoke with God,
Nor visited in heaven;
Yet certain am I of the spot
As if the chart were given.

———

Superfluous were the sun
  When excellence is dead;
He were superfluous every day,
  For every day is said

That syllable whose faith
  Just saves it from despair,
And whose "I'll meet you" hesitates—
  If love inquire, "Where?"

Upon his dateless fame
  Our periods may lie,
As stars that drop anonymous
  From an abundant sky.

———

How still the bells in steeples stand,
  Till, swollen with the sky,
They leap upon their silver feet
  In frantic melody!

———

Let down the bars, O Death!
The tired flocks come in
Whose bleating ceases to repeat,
Whose wandering is done.

Thine is the stillest night,
Thine the securest fold;
Too near thou art for seeking thee,
Too tender to be told.

———

Nature rarer uses yellow
    Than another hue;
Saves she all of that for sunsets,—
    Prodigal of blue,

Spending scarlet like a woman,
    Yellow she affords
Only scantly and selectly,
    Like a lover's words.

———

To help our bleaker parts
    Salubrious hours are given,
Which if they do not fit for earth
    Drill silently for heaven.

———

A narrow fellow in the grass
Occasionally rides;
You may have met him,—did you not?
His notice sudden is.

The grass divides as with a comb,
A spotted shaft is seen;
And then it closes at your feet
And opens further on.

He likes a boggy acre,
A floor too cool for corn.
Yet when a child, and barefoot,
I more than once, at morn,

Have passed, I thought, a whip-lash
Unbraiding in the sun,—
When, stooping to secure it,
It wrinkled, and was gone.

Several of nature's people
I know, and they know me;
I feel for them a transport
Of cordiality;

But never met this fellow,
Attended or alone,
Without a tighter breathing,
And zero at the bone.

———

That such have died enables us
  The tranquiller to die;
That such have lived, certificate
  For immortality.

———

The stimulus, beyond the grave
  His countenance to see,
Supports me like imperial drams
  Afforded royally.

———

I had a daily bliss
  I half indifferent viewed,
Till sudden I perceived it stir,—
  It grew as I pursued,

Till when, around a crag,
    It wasted from my sight,
Enlarged beyond my utmost scope,
    I learned its sweetness right.

———

The dying need but little, dear,—
    A glass of water's all,
A flower's unobtrusive face
    To punctuate the wall,

A fan, perhaps, a friend's regret,
    And certainly that one
No color in the rainbow
    Perceives when you are gone.

———

The leaves, like women, interchange
    Sagacious confidence;
Somewhat of nods, and somewhat of
    Portentous inference,

The parties in both cases
    Enjoining secrecy,—
Inviolable compact
    To notoriety.

———

Fate slew him, but he did not drop;
    She felled—he did not fall—
Impaled him on her fiercest stakes—
    He neutralized them all.

She stung him, sapped his firm advance,
    But, when her worst was done,
And he, unmoved, regarded her,
    Acknowledged him a man.

———

Far from love the Heavenly Father
    Leads the chosen child;
Oftener through realm of briar
    Than the meadow mild,

Oftener by the claw of dragon
    Than the hand of friend,
Guides the little one predestined
    To the native land.

———

This was in the white of the year,
    That was in the green,
Drifts were as difficult then to think
    As daisies now to be seen.

Looking back is best that is left,
    Or if it be before,
Retrospection is prospect's half,
    Sometimes almost more.

———

Three weeks passed since I had seen her,—
    Some disease had vexed;
'Twas with text and village singing
    I beheld her next,

And a company—our pleasure
    To discourse alone;
Gracious now to me as any,
    Gracious unto none.

Borne, without dissent of either,
    To the parish night;
Of the separated people
    Which are out of sight?

Just once—oh least request!
Could adamant refuse
So small a grace,
So scanty put,
Such agonizing terms?

Would not a God of flint
Be conscious of a sigh,
As down his heaven dropt remote,
"Just once, sweet Deity?"

We learn in the retreating
    How vast an one
Was recently among us.
    A perished sun

Endears in the departure
    How doubly more
Than all the golden presence
    It was before!

The bustle in a house
The morning after death
Is solemnest of industries
Enacted upon earth,—

The sweeping up the heart,
And putting love away
We shall not want to use again
Until eternity.

———

My cocoon tightens, colors tease,
I'm feeling for the air;
A dim capacity for wings
Degrades the dress I wear.

A power of butterfly must be
The aptitude to fly,
Meadows of majesty concedes
And easy sweeps of sky.

So I must baffle at the hint
And cipher at the sign,
And make much blunder, if at last
I take the clew divine.

———

The sky is low, the clouds are mean,
A travelling flake of snow
Across a barn or through a rut
Debates if it will go.

A narrow wind complains all day
How some one treated him;
Nature, like us, is sometimes caught
Without her diadem.

———

Superiority to fate
    Is difficult to learn.
'Tis not conferred by any,
    But possible to earn

A pittance at a time,
  Until, to her surprise,
The soul with strict economy
  Subsists till Paradise.

————

The last night that she lived,
It was a common night,
Except the dying; this to us
Made nature different.

We noticed smallest things,—
Things overlooked before,
By this great light upon our minds
Italicized, as 'twere.

That others could exist
While she must finish quite,
A jealousy for her arose
So nearly infinite.

We waited while she passed;
It was a narrow time,
Too jostled were our souls to speak,
At length the notice came.

She mentioned, and forgot;
Then lightly as a reed
Bent to the water, shivered scarce,
Consented, and was dead.

And we, we placed the hair,
And drew the head erect;
And then an awful leisure was,
Our faith to regulate.

————

At half-past three a single bird
Unto a silent sky
Propounded but a single term
Of cautious melody.

At half-past four, experiment
Had subjugated test,
And lo! her silver principle
Supplanted all the rest.

At half-past seven, element
Nor implement was seen,
And place was where the presence was,
Circumference between.

———

Farther in summer than the birds,
Pathetic from the grass,
A minor nation celebrates
Its unobtrusive mass.

No ordinance is seen,
So gradual the grace,
A pensive custom it becomes,
Enlarging loneliness.

Antiquest felt at noon
When August, burning low,
Calls forth this spectral canticle,
Repose to typify.

Remit as yet no grace,
No furrow on the glow,
Yet a druidic difference
Enhances nature now.

———

The cricket sang,
    And set the sun,
And workmen finished, one by one,
    Their seam the day upon.

The low grass loaded with the dew,
The twilight stood as strangers do
With hat in hand, polite and new,
    To stay as if, or go.

A vastness, as a neighbor, came,—
A wisdom without face or name,
A peace, as hemispheres at home,—
    And so the night became.

————

After a hundred years
Nobody knows the place,—
Agony, that enacted there,
Motionless as peace.

Weeds triumphant ranged,
Strangers strolled and spelled
At the lone orthography
Of the elder dead.

Winds of summer fields
Recollect the way,—
Instinct picking up the key
Dropped by memory.

————

A spider sewed at night
Without a light
Upon an arc of white.

If ruff it was of dame
Or shroud of gnome,
Himself, himself inform.
Of immortality
His strategy
Was physiognomy.

———

I noticed people disappeared,
When but a little child,—
Supposed they visited remote,
Or settled regions wild.

Now know I they both visited
And settled regions wild,
But did because they died,—a fact
Withheld the little child!

———

Great streets of silence led away
To neighborhoods of pause;
Here was no notice, no dissent,
No universe, no laws.

By clocks 'twas morning, and for night
The bells at distance called;
But epoch had no basis here,
For period exhaled.

———

We never know how high we are
    Till we are called to rise;
And then, if we are true to plan,
    Our statures touch the skies.

The heroism we recite
  Would be a daily thing,
Did not ourselves the cubits warp
  For fear to be a king.

———

The clouds their backs together laid,
The north begun to push,
The forests galloped till they fell,
The lightning skipped like mice;
The thunder crumbled like a stuff—
How good to be safe in tombs,
Where nature's temper cannot reach,
Nor vengeance ever comes!

———

When I hoped I feared,
Since I hoped I dared;
Everywhere alone
As a church remain;
Spectre cannot harm,
Serpent cannot charm;
He deposes doom,
Who hath suffered him.

———

Remembrance has a rear and front,—
  'Tis something like a house;
It has a garret also
  For refuse and the mouse,

Besides, the deepest cellar
  That ever mason hewed;
Look to it, by its fathoms
  Ourselves be not pursued.

———

Step lightly on this narrow spot!
The broadest land that grows
Is not so ample as the breast
These emerald seams enclose.

Step lofty; for this name is told
As far as cannon dwell,
Or flag subsist, or fame export
Her deathless syllable.

———

The past is such a curious creature,
    To look her in the face
A transport may reward us,
    Or a disgrace.

Unarmed if any meet her,
    I charge him, fly!
Her rusty ammunition
    Might yet reply!

———

Are friends delight or pain?
Could bounty but remain
    Riches were good.

But if they only stay
Bolder to fly away,
    Riches are sad.

———

Immortal is an ample word
    When what we need is by,
But when it leaves us for a time,
    'Tis a necessity.

Of heaven above the firmest proof
   We fundamental know,
Except for its marauding hand,
   It had been heaven below.

———.

A deed knocks first at thought,
And then it knocks at will.
That is the manufacturing spot,
And will at home and well.

It then goes out an act,
Or is entombed so still
That only to the ear of God
Its doom is audible.

———

Given in marriage unto thee,
   Oh, thou celestial host!
Bride of the Father and the Son,
   Bride of the Holy Ghost!

———

Other betrothal shall dissolve,
   Wedlock of will decay;
Only the keeper of this seal
   Conquers mortality.

———

He preached upon "breadth" till it argued him
   narrow,—
The broad are too broad to define;
And of "truth" until it proclaimed him a liar,—
The truth never flaunted a sign.

Simplicity fled from his counterfeit presence
As gold the pyrites would shun.
What confusion would cover the innocent Jesus
To meet so enabled a man!

———

The show is not the show,
But they that go.
Menagerie to me
My neighbor be.
Fair play—
Both went to see.

———

So proud she was to die
  It made us all ashamed
That what we cherished, so unknown
  To her desire seemed.

So satisfied to go
  Where none of us should be,
Immediately, that anguish stooped
  Almost to jealousy.

———

While I was fearing it, it came,
  But came with less of fear,
Because that fearing it so long
  Had almost made it dear.
There is a fitting a dismay,
  A fitting a despair.

'Tis harder knowing it is due,
  Than knowing it is here.
The trying on the utmost,
  The morning it is new,
Is terribler than wearing it
  A whole existence through.

————

There is no frigate like a book
  To take us lands away,
Nor any coursers like a page
  Of prancing poetry.

This traverse may the poorest take
  Without oppress of toll;
How frugal is the chariot
  That bears a human soul!

————

The butterfly's assumption-gown,
In chrysoprase apartments hung,
  This afternoon put on.

How condescending to descend,
And be of buttercups the friend
  In a New England town!

————

The spider as an artist
  Has never been employed
Though his surpassing merit
  Is freely certified

By every broom and Bridget
    Throughout a Christian land.
Neglected son of genius,
    I take thee by the hand.

―――

Is Heaven a physician?
    They say that He can heal;
But medicine posthumous
    Is unavailable.

Is Heaven an exchequer?
    They speak of what we owe;
But that negotiation
    I'm not a party to.

―――

The mushroom is the elf of plants,
At evening it is not;
At morning in a truffled hut
It stops upon a spot

As if it tarried always;
And yet its whole career
Is shorter than a snake's delay,
And fleeter than a tare.

'Tis vegetation's juggler,
The germ of alibi;
Doth like a bubble antedate,
And like a bubble hie.

I feel as if the grass were pleased
To have it intermit;
The surreptitious scion
Of summer's circumspect.

Had nature any outcast face,
Could she a son contemn,
Had nature an Iscariot,
That mushroom,—it is him.

———

That short, potential stir
That each can make but once,
That bustle so illustrious
'Tis almost consequence,

Is the *éclat* of death.
Oh, thou unknown renown
That not a beggar would accept,
Had he the power to spurn!

———

Dear March, come in!
How glad I am!
I looked for you before.
Put down your hat—
You must have walked—
How out of breath you are!
Dear March, how are you?
And the rest?
Did you leave Nature well?
Oh, March, come right upstairs with me,
I have so much to tell!

I got your letter, and the bird's;
The maples never knew
That you were coming,—I declare,
How red their faces grew!

But, March, forgive me—
And all those hills
You left for me to hue;
There was no purple suitable,
You took it all with you.

Who knocks? That April!
Lock the door!
I will not be pursued!
He stayed away a year, to call
When I am occupied.
But trifles look so trivial
As soon as you have come,
That blame is just as dear as praise
And praise as mere as blame.

———

Let me not mar that perfect dream
    By an auroral stain,
But so adjust my daily night
    That it will come again.

———

(With the first Arbutus.)

Pink, small, and punctual,
Aromatic, low,
Covert in April,
Candid in May,

Dear to the moss,
Known by the knoll,
Next to the robin
In every human soul.

Bold little beauty,
Bedecked with thee,
Nature forswears
Antiquity.

———

The rat is the concisest tenant.
He pays no rent,—
Repudiates the obligation,
On schemes intent.

Balking our wit
To sound or circumvent,
Hate cannot harm
A foe so reticent.

Neither decree
Prohibits him,
Lawful as
Equilibrium.

———

Forbidden fruit a flavor has
    That lawful orchards mocks;
How luscious lies the pea within
    The pod that Duty locks!

———

The bat is dun with wrinkled wings
    Like fallow article,
And not a song pervades his lips,
    Or none perceptible.

His small umbrella, quaintly halved,
    Describing in the air
An arc alike inscrutable,—
    Elate philosopher!

Deputed from what firmament
  Of what astute abode,
Empowered with what malevolence
  Auspiciously withheld.

To his adroit Creator
  Ascribe no less the praise;
Beneficent, believe me,
  His eccentricities.

———

She laid her docile crescent down,
  And this mechanic stone
Still states, to dates that have forgot,
  The news that she is gone.

So constant to its stolid trust,
  The shaft that never knew,
It shames the constancy that fled
  Before its emblem flew.

———

It sounded as if the streets were running,
And then the streets stood still.
Eclipse was all we could see at the window,
And awe was all we could feel.

By and by the boldest stole out of his covert,
To see if time was there.
Nature was in her beryl apron,
Mixing fresher air.

———

What mystery pervades a well!
   The water lives so far,
Like neighbor from another world
   Residing in a jar.

The grass does not appear afraid;
   I often wonder he
Can stand so close and look so bold
   At what is dread to me.

Related somehow they may be,—
   The sedge stands next the sea,
Where he is floorless, yet of fear
   No evidence gives he.

But nature is a stranger yet;
   The ones that cite her most
Have never passed her haunted house,
   Nor simplified her ghost.

To pity those that know her not
   Is helped by the regret
That those who know her, know her less
   The nearer her they get.

———

Could mortal lip divine
   The undeveloped freight
Of a delivered syllable,
   'Twould crumble with the weight.

———

I have no life but this,
To lead it here;
Nor any death, but lest
Dispelled from there;

Nor tie to earths to come,
Nor action new,
Except through this extent,
The realm of you.

———

Lay this laurel on the one
Too intrinsic for renown.
Laurel! veil your deathless tree,—
Him you chasten, that is he!

———

Belshazzar had a letter,—
He never had but one;
Belshazzar's correspondent
Concluded and begun
In that immortal copy
The conscience of us all
Can read without its glasses
On revelation's wall.

———

Before you thought of spring,
Except as a surmise,
You see, God bless his suddenness,
A fellow in the skies
Of independent hues,
A little weather-worn,
Inspiriting habiliments
Of indigo and brown.

With specimens of song,
As if for you to choose,
Discretion in the interval,
With gay delays he goes

To some superior tree
Without a single leaf,
And shouts for joy to nobody
But his seraphic self!

———

One of the ones that Midas touched,
Who failed to touch us all,
Was that confiding prodigal,
The blissful oriole.

So drunk, he disavows it
With badinage divine;
So dazzling, we mistake him
For an alighting mine.

A pleader, a dissembler,
An epicure, a thief,—
Betimes an oratorio,
An ecstasy in chief;

The Jesuit of orchards,
He cheats as he enchants
Of an entire attar
For his decamping wants.

The splendor of a Burmah,
The meteor of birds,
Departing like a pageant
Of ballads and of bards.

I never thought that Jason sought
For any golden fleece;
But then I am a rural man,
With thoughts that make for peace.

But if there were a Jason,
Tradition suffer me
Behold his lost emolument
Upon the apple-tree.

———

Look back on time with kindly eyes,
He doubtless did his best;
How softly sinks his trembling sun
In human nature's west!

———

'Tis whiter than an Indian pipe,
    'Tis dimmer than a lace;
No stature has it, like a fog,
    When you approach the place.

Not any voice denotes it here,
    Or intimates it there;
A spirit, how doth it accost?
    What customs hath the air?

This limitless hyperbole
    Each one of us shall be;
'Tis drama, if (hypothesis)
    It be not tragedy!

———

A route of evanescence
With a revolving wheel;
A resonance of emerald,
A rush of cochineal;
And every blossom on the bush
Adjusts its tumbled head,—
The mail from Tunis, probably,
An easy morning's ride.

———

The robin is a Gabriel
In humble circumstances,
His dress denotes him socially
Of transport's working classes.
He has the punctuality
Of a New England farmer—
The same oblique integrity,
A vista vastly warmer.
A small but sturdy residence,
A self-denying household,
The guests of perspicacity
Are all that cross his threshold.
As covert as a fugitive,
Cajoling consternation
By ditties to the enemy,
And sylvan punctuation.

———

Mine enemy is growing old,—
I have at last revenge.
The palate of the hate departs;
If any would avenge,—

Let him be quick, the viand flits,
It is a faded meat.
Anger as soon as fed is dead;
'Tis starving makes it fat.

———

How happy is the little stone
That rambles in the road alone,
And doesn't care about careers,
And exigencies never fears;
Whose coat of elemental brown

A passing universe put on;
And independent as the sun,
Associates or glows alone,
Fulfilling absolute decree
In casual simplicity.

———

From all the jails the boys and girls
    Ecstatically leap,—
Beloved, only afternoon
    That prison doesn't keep.

They storm the earth and stun the air,
    A mob of solid bliss.
Alas! that frowns could lie in wait
    For such a foe as this!

———

We never know we go,—when we are going
    We jest and shut the door;
Fate following behind us bolts it,
    And we accost no more.

———

As imperceptibly as grief
The summer lapsed away,—
Too imperceptible, at last,
To seem like perfidy.

A quietness distilled,
As twilight long begun,
Or Nature, spending with herself
Sequestered afternoon.

The dusk drew earlier in,
The morning foreign shone,—
A courteous, yet harrowing grace,
As guest who would be gone.

And thus, without a wing,
Or service of a keel,
Our summer made her light escape
Into the beautiful.

———

Hope is a subtle glutton;
　He feeds upon the fair;
And yet, inspected closely,
　What abstinence is there!

His is the halcyon table
　That never seats but one,
And whatsoever is consumed
　The same amounts remain.

———

No brigadier throughout the year
So civic as the Jay.
A neighbor and a warrior too,
With shrill felicity

Pursuing winds that censure us
A February day,
The brother of the universe
Was never blown away.

The snow and he are intimate;
I've often seen them play
When heaven looked upon us all
With such severity,

I felt apology were due
To an insulted sky,
Whose pompous frown was nutriment
To their temerity.

The pillow of this daring head
Is pungent evergreens;
His larder—terse and militant—
Unknown, refreshing things;

His character a tonic,
His future a dispute;
Unfair an immortality
That leaves this neighbor out.

———

Who has not found the heaven below
    Will fail of it above.
God's residence is next to mine,
    His furniture is love.

———

There came a wind like a bugle;
It quivered through the grass,
And a green chill upon the heat
So ominous did pass
We barred the windows and the doors
As from an emerald ghost;
The doom's electric moccasin
That very instant passed.
On a strange mob of panting trees,
And fences fled away,
And rivers where the houses ran
The living looked that day.

The bell within the steeple wild
The flying tidings whirled.
How much can come
And much can go,
And yet abide the world!

———

The farthest thunder that I heard
    Was nearer than the sky,
And rumbles still, though torrid noons
    Have lain their missiles by.
The lightning that preceded it
    Struck no one but myself,
But I would not exchange the bolt
    For all the rest of life.
Indebtedness to oxygen
    The chemist may repay,
But not the obligation
    To electricity.
It founds the homes and decks the days,
    And every clamor bright
Is but the gleam concomitant
    Of that waylaying light.
The thought is quiet as a flake,—
    A crash without a sound;
How life's reverberation
    Its explanation found!

———

He ate and drank the precious words,
His spirit grew robust;
He knew no more that he was poor,
Nor that his frame was dust.

He danced along the dingy days,
And this bequest of wings
Was but a book. What liberty
A loosened spirit brings!

Apparently with no surprise
To any happy flower,
The frost beheads it at its play
In accidental power.

The blond assassin passes on,
The sun proceeds unmoved
To measure off another day
For an approving God.

Not knowing when the dawn will come
    I open every door;
Or has it feathers like a bird,
    Or billows like a shore?

My life closed twice before its close;
    It yet remains to see
If Immortality unveil
    A third event to me,

So huge, so hopeless to conceive,
    As these that twice befell.
Parting is all we know of heaven,
    And all we need of hell.

The distance that the dead have gone
  Does not at first appear;
Their coming back seems possible
  For many an ardent year.

And then, that we have followed them
  We more than half suspect,
So intimate have we become
  With their dear retrospect.

———

The reticent volcano keeps
  His never slumbering plan;
Confided are his projects pink
  To no precarious man.

If nature will not tell the tale
  Jehovah told to her,
Can human nature not survive
  Without a listener?

Admonished by her buckled lips
  Let every babbler be.
The only secret people keep
  Is Immortality.

———

Sweet is the swamp with its secrets,
  Until we meet a snake;
Tis then we sigh for houses,
  And our departure take

At that enthralling gallop
  That only childhood knows.
A snake is summer's treason,
  And guile is where it goes.

———

High from the earth I heard a bird;
   He trod upon the trees
As he esteemed them trifles,
   And then he spied a breeze,
And situated softly
   Upon a pile of wind
Which in a perturbation
   Nature had left behind.
A joyous-going fellow
   I gathered from his talk,
Which both of benediction
   And badinage partook,
Without apparent burden,
   I learned, in leafy wood
He was the faithful father
   Of a dependent brood;
And this untoward transport
   His remedy for care,—
A contrast to our respites.
   How different we are!

———

Elysium is as far as to
The very nearest room,
If in that room a friend await
Felicity or doom.

What fortitude the soul contains,
That it can so endure
The accent of a coming foot,
The opening of a door!

———

A train went through a burial gate,
A bird broke forth and sang,
And trilled, and quivered, and shook his throat
Till all the churchyard rang;

And then adjusted his little notes,
And bowed and sang again.
Doubtless, he thought it meet of him
To say good-by to men.

———

Death is like the insect
   Menacing the tree,
Competent to kill it,
   But decoyed may be.

Bait it with the balsam,
   Seek it with the knife,
Baffle, if it cost you
   Everything in life.

Then, if it have burrowed
   Out of reach of skill,
Ring the tree and leave it,—
   'Tis the vermin's will.

———

How dare the robins sing,
   When men and women hear
Who since they went to their account
   Have settled with the year!—
Paid all that life had earned
   In one consummate bill,
And now, what life or death can do
   Is immaterial.
Insulting is the sun
   To him whose mortal light,
Beguiled of immortality,
   Bequeaths him to the night.

In deference to him
    Extinct be every hum,
Whose garden wrestles with the dew,
    At daybreak overcome!

———

Sweet hours have perished here;
    This is a mighty room;
Within its precincts hopes have played,—
    Now shadows in the tomb.

———

Proud of my broken heart since thou didst break it,
    Proud of the pain I did not feel till thee,
Proud of my night since thou with moons dost slake it,
    Not to partake thy passion, my humility.

———

Drowning is not so pitiful
    As the attempt to rise.
Three times, 'tis said, a sinking man
    Comes up to face the skies,
And then declines forever
    To that abhorred abode

Where hope and he part company,—
    For he is grasped of God.
The Maker's cordial visage,
    However good to see,
Is shunned, we must admit it,
    Like an adversity.

———

To lose thee, sweeter than to gain
    All other hearts I knew.
'Tis true the drought is destitute,
    But then I had the dew!

The Caspian has its realms of sand,
    Its other realm of sea;
Without the sterile perquisite
    No Caspian could be.

———

A face devoid of love or grace,
A hateful, hard, successful face,
    A face with which a stone
Would feel as thoroughly at ease
As were they old acquaintances,—
    First time together thrown.

———

To make a prairie it takes a clover and one bee,—
One clover, and a bee,
And revery.
The revery alone will do
If bees are few.

———

Softened by Time's consummate plush,
    How sleek the woe appears
That threatened childhood's citadel
    And undermined the years!

Bisected now by bleaker griefs,
    We envy the despair
That devastated childhood's realm,
    So easy to repair.

——

The grave my little cottage is,
    Where, keeping house for thee,
I make my parlor orderly,
    And lay the marble tea,

For two divided, briefly,
    A cycle, it may be,
Till everlasting life unite
    In strong society.

——

SELECTED LETTERS

WITH BIOGRAPHICAL NOTES
ON THE RECIPIENTS

*My life has been too simple and
stern to embarrass any.*

Directory of Recipients

ELBRIDGE G. BOWDOIN was a young lawyer who, at the time E.D. sent him a valentine, was working in her father's office.

SAMUEL BOWLES, editor of the Springfield *Republican*, was an old and valued family friend. There are extant about fifty letters of E.D. to Mr. Bowles and his wife, MARY BOWLES.

JOSEPH K. CHICKERING taught English at Amherst College.

JAMES D. CLARK was a close friend of Charles Wadsworth, the clergyman who was E.D.'s "shepherd" and "dearest earthly friend." On Wadsworth's death they exchanged memories of him, and when James D. Clark became fatally ill E.D. transferred the correspondence to his brother, CHARLES H. CLARK.

PEREZ DICKINSON COWAN, "Cousin Peter" to E.D., had been her friend while a student at Amherst College and later corresponded with her while a clergyman in various parts of the country.

LAVINIA DICKINSON, E.D.'s sister, lived with her throughout her life.

WILLIAM AUSTIN DICKINSON was E.D.'s beloved brother. The earlier letters were written while she was a student at Mount Holyoke Seminary, letters of 1851 and 1852 while he was teaching school in Boston, and those of 1853 and 1854 while he studied law at Harvard. He married Susan Gilbert in 1856 and practiced law in Amherst for the rest of his life.

THOMAS WENTWORTH HIGGINSON. The choicest of E.D.'s letters to Higginson are quoted in his essay at the beginning of this book. For biographical information see the note preceding the essay.

DR. and MRS. JOSIAH GILBERT HOLLAND were among E.D.'s closest friends. Dr. Holland was on the staff of the Springfield *Republican* and, later, editor of *Scribner's Monthly*. E.D. sometimes addressed Mrs. Holland as Sister.

WILLIAM HOWLAND, a law student in the office of Edward Dickinson, was the recipient of a droll valentine from E.D., which was published anonymously in the *Republican*.

SALLY JENKINS was the wife of Jonathan L. Jenkins, pastor of the First Church of Amherst.

LOUISE and FANNIE NORCROSS, the "Little Cousins" of E.D., were frequent visitors at the Dickinson home. E.D. stayed with them in Cambridge when she was being treated by a Boston eye doctor in 1864 and 1865.

ABIAH ROOT was a school friend with whom E.D. corresponded until her marriage to the Rev. Samuel W. Strong in 1854. The initial E., which E.D. used in these early letters, stood for Elizabeth, a middle name soon discarded.

MABEL LOOMIS TODD, wife of the professor of astronomy at Amherst, was the first editor of E.D.'s poems and letters.

MRS. EDWARD TUCKERMAN was wife of the professor of botany at Amherst.

MRS. KATE SCOTT TURNER met E.D. while visiting Sue Dickinson in 1859. The correspondence ceased after her marriage to John Anthon in 1866.

UNKNOWN RECIPIENTS. These letters are first drafts found among E.D.'s papers. The one tentatively dated 1861 was probably to the Rev. Charles Wadsworth. There is no clue to the other.

MARIA WHITNEY of Northampton was related to the Bowles family and was a Dickinson family friend.

The letters that follow are arranged in an approximation to chronological order, but since Emily Dickinson seldom used dates after 1850 this has been determined by postmarks, internal references, and handwriting, and is, therefore, often conjectural.

To *Abiah Root*
[When Emily was fourteen]

Amherst, Feb. 23, 1845

Dear Abiah,—After receiving the smitings of conscience for a
long time, I have at length succeeded in stifling the voice of
that faithful monitor by a promise of a long letter to you; so
leave everything and sit down prepared for a long siege in the
shape of a bundle of nonsense from friend E.
. . . I keep your lock of hair as precious as gold and a
great deal more so. I often look at it when I go to my little lot
of treasures, and wish the owner of that glossy lock were
here. Old Time wags on pretty much as usual at Amherst,
and I know of nothing that has occurred to break the silence;
however, the reduction of the postage has excited my risibles
somewhat. Only think! We can send a letter before long for
five little coppers only, filled with the thoughts and advice of
dear friends. But I will not get into a philosophizing strain
just yet. There is time enough for that upon another page of
this mammoth sheet. . . . Your *beau idéal* D. I have not
seen lately. I presume he was changed into a star some night
while gazing at them, and placed in the constellation Orion
between Bellatrix and Betelgeux. I doubt not if he was here
he would wish to be kindly remembered to you. What de-
lightful weather we have had for a week! . . .
I wish you would come and make me a long visit. If you

will, I will entertain you to the best of my abilities, which you know are neither few nor small. Why can't you persuade your father and mother to let you come here to school next term, and keep me company, as I am going? Miss ——, I presume you can guess who I mean, is going to finish her education next summer. The finishing stroke is to be put on at Newton. She will then have learned all that we poor foot-travellers are toiling up the hill of knowledge to acquire. Wonderful thought! Her horse has carried her along so swiftly that she has nearly gained the summit, and we are plodding along on foot after her. Well said and sufficient this. We'll finish an education sometime, won't we? You may then be Plato, and I will be Socrates, provided you won't be wiser than I am. Lavinia just now interrupted my flow of thought by saying give my love to A. I presume you will be glad to have some one break off this epistle. All the girls send much love to you. And please accept a large share for yourself.

From your beloved
Emily E. Dickinson

Please send me a copy of that Romance you were writing at Amherst. I am in a fever to read it. I expect it will be against my Whig feelings.

To Abiah Root

Amherst, May 7, 1845

Dear Abiah,—It seems almost an age since I have seen you, and it is indeed an age for friends to be separated. I was delighted to receive a paper from you, and I also was much pleased with the news it contained, especially that you are taking lessons on the "piny," as you always call it. But remember not to get on ahead of me. Father intends to have a piano very soon. How happy I shall be when I have one of my own! Old Father Time has wrought many changes here since your last short visit. Miss S. T. and Miss N. M. have both taken the marriage vows upon themselves. Dr. Hitchcock has moved into his new house, and Mr. Tyler across the way from our house has moved into President Hitchcock's old house. Mr. C. is going to move into Mr. T.'s former house, but the worst thing old Time has done here is he has walked so fast as to overtake H. M. and carry her to Hartford on last week Saturday. I was so vexed with him for it that I ran after him and made out to get near enough to him to put some salt on his tail, when he fled and left me to run home alone. . . . Viny went to Boston this morning with father, to be gone a fortnight, and I am left alone in all my glory. I suppose she has got there before this time, and is probably staring with mouth and eyes wide open at the wonders of the city. I have been to walk to-night, and got some very choice wild flowers. I wish you had some of them. Viny and I both go to school this term. We have a very fine school. There are 63 scholars. I have four studies. They are Mental Philosophy, Geology, Latin, and Botany. How large they sound, don't they? I don't believe you have such big studies. . . . My plants look finely now. I am going to send you a little geranium leaf in this letter, which you must press for me. Have you made you an herbarium yet? I hope you will if you have not, it would be such a treasure to you; 'most all the girls are making one. If you do, perhaps I can make some additions to it from flowers growing around here. How do you enjoy your school this term? Are the teachers as pleasant as our old school-teachers? I expect you have a great many prim, starched up young ladies there, who, I doubt not, are perfect models of propriety and good behavior. If they are, don't let your free spirit be chained by them. I don't know as there [are] any in school of this stamp. But there 'most always are a few, whom the teachers look up to and regard as their satellites. I am growing handsome very fast indeed! I expect I shall be the belle of Amherst when I reach my 17th year. I don't doubt that I shall have perfect crowds of admirers at that age. Then how I shall delight to make them await my bidding, and with what delight shall I witness their suspense while I make my final decision. But away with my nonsense. I have written one composition this term, and I need not assure you it was exceedingly edifying to myself as well as everybody else. Don't you want to see it? I really wish you could have a chance. We are obliged to write compositions once in a fortnight, and select a piece to read from some interesting book the week that we don't write compositions. We really have some most charming young women in school this term. I shan't call them anything but women, for women they are in every sense of the word. I must, however, describe one, and while I describe her I wish Imagination, who is ever present with you, to make a little picture of this self-same young lady in your mind, and by her aid see if you cannot conceive how she looks. Well, to begin. . . . Then just imagine her as she is, and a huge string of gold beads encircling her neck, and don't she present a lively picture; and then she is so bustling, she is always whizzing about, and whenever I come in contact with her I really think I am in a hornet's nest. I can't help thinking every time I see this singular piece of humanity of Shakespeare's description of a tempest in a teapot. But I must not laugh about her, for I verily believe she has a good heart, and that is the principal thing now-a-days. Don't you hope I shall become wiser in the company of such virtuosos? It would certainly be desirable. Have you noticed how beautifully the trees look now? They seem to be completely covered with fragrant blossoms. . . . I had so many things to do for Viny, as she was going away, that very much against my wishes I deferred writing you until now, but forgive and forget, dear A., and I will promise to do better in future. Do write me soon, and let it be a long, long letter; and when you can't get time to write, send a paper, so as to let me know you think of me still, though we are separated by hill and stream. All the girls send much love to you. Don't forget to let me receive a letter from you soon. I can say no more now as my paper is all filled up.

Your affectionate friend
Emily E. Dickinson

To Abiah Root

My Dear Friend Abiah,—It is a long, long time since I received your welcome letter, and it becomes me to sue for forgiveness, which I am sure your affectionate heart will not refuse to grant. But many and unforeseen circumstances have caused my long delay. . . . Father and mother thought a journey would be of service to me, and accordingly I left for Boston week before last. I had a delightful ride in the cars, and am now getting settled down, if there can be such a state in the city. I am visiting in my aunt's family, and am happy. "Happy," did I say? No; not happy, but contented. I have been here a fortnight today, and in that time I have both seen and heard a great many wonderful things. Perhaps you might like to know how I have spent my time here. I have been to Mount Auburn, to the Chinese Museum, to Bunker Hill; I have attended two concerts and one Horticultural Exhibition. I have been upon the top of the State House, and almost everywhere that you can imagine. Have you ever been to Mount Auburn? If not, you can form but slight conception of this "City of the Dead." It seems as if nature had formed this spot with a distinct idea in view of its being a resting-place for her children, where, wearied and disappointed, they might stretch themselves beneath the spreading cypress, and close their eyes "calmly as to a night's repose, or flowers at set of sun" . . .

Does it seem as though September had come? How swiftly summer has fled, and what report has it borne to heaven of misspent time and wasted hours? Eternity only will answer. The ceaseless flight of the seasons is to me a very solemn thought; and yet why do we not strive to make a better improvement of them? With how much emphasis the poet has said, "We take no note of time but from its loss. 'Twere wise in men to give it then a tongue. Pay no moment but in just purchase of its worth, and what it's worth, ask death-beds. They can tell. Part with it, as with life, reluctantly." Then we have higher authority than that of man for the improvement of our time. For God has said, "Work while the day lasts, for the night is coming in the which no man can work. . . ."

Your affectionate friend,
Emily E. D.

To William Austin Dickinson
[South Hadley, autumn, 1847]

My dear Brother Austin,—I have not really a moment of time in which to write you, and am taking time from "silent study hours"; but I am determined not to break my promise again, and I generally carry my resolutions into effect. I watched you until you were out of sight Saturday evening, and then went to my room and looked over my treasures; and surely no miser ever counted his heaps of gold with more satisfaction than I gazed upon the presents from home. . . .

I can't tell you now how much good your visit did me. My spirits have wonderfully lightened since then. I had a great mind to be homesick after you went home, but I concluded not to, and therefore gave up all homesick feelings. Was not that a wise determination? . . .

There has been a menagerie here this week. Miss Lyon provided "Daddy Hawks" as a beau for all the Seminary girls who wished to see the bears and monkeys, and your sister, not caring to go, was obliged to decline the gallantry of said gentleman,—which I fear I may never have another opportunity to avail myself of. The whole company stopped in front of the Seminary and played for about a quarter of an hour, for the purpose of getting custom in the afternoon, I opine. Almost all the girls went; and I enjoyed the solitude finely.

I want to know when you are coming to see me again, for I want to see you as much as I did before. I went to see Miss F. in her room yesterday. . . . I love her very much, and think I shall love all the teachers when I become better acquainted with them and find out their ways, which, I can assure you, are almost "past finding out."

I had almost forgotten to tell you of a dream which I dreamed last night, and I would like to have you turn Daniel and interpret it to me; or if you don't care about going through all the perils which he did, I will allow you to interpret it without, provided you will try to tell no lies about it. Well, I dreamed a dream, and lo! father had failed, and mother said that "our rye-field, which she and I planted, was mortaged to Seth Nims." I hope it is not true; but do write soon and tell me, for you know I should expire of mortification to have our rye-field mortgaged, to say nothing of its falling into the merciless hands of a loco!

Won't you please to tell me when you answer my letter who the candidate for President is? I have been trying to find out ever since I came here, and have not yet succeeded. I don't know anything more about affairs in the world than if I were in a trance, and you must imagine with all your "Sophomoric discernment" that it is but little and very faint. Has the Mexican War terminated yet, and how? Are we beaten? Do you know of any nation about to besiege South Hadley? If so, do inform me of it, for I would be glad of a chance to escape, if we are to be stormed. I suppose Miss Lyon would furnish us all with daggers and order us to fight for our lives in case such perils should befall us. . . . Miss F. told me if I was writing to Amherst to send her love. Not specifying to whom, you may deal it out as your good sense and discretion prompt. Be a good boy and mind me!

Your aff. Emily

Mount Holyoke Seminary
Nov. 6, 1847

My dear Abiah,—I am really at Mount Holyoke Seminary
and this is to be my home for a long year. Your affectionate
letter was joyfully received, and I wish that this might make
you as happy as yours did me. It has been nearly six weeks
since I left home, and that is a longer time than I was ever
away from home before now. I was very homesick for a few
days, and it seemed to me I could not live here. But I am now
contented and quite happy, if I can be happy when absent
from my dear home and friends. You may laugh at the idea
that I cannot be happy when away from home, but you must
remember that I have a very dear home and that this is my
first trial in the way of absence for any length of time in my
life. As you desire it, I will give you a full account of myself
since I first left the paternal roof. I came to South Hadley six
weeks ago next Thursday. I was much fatigued with the ride,
and had a severe cold besides, which prevented me from
commencing my examinations until the next day, when I be-
gan. I finished them in three days, and found them about
what I had anticipated, though the old scholars say they are
more strict than they ever have been before. As you can eas-
ily imagine, I was much delighted to finish without failures,
and I came to the conclusion then, that I should not be at all
homesick, but the reaction left me as homesick a girl as it is
not usual to see. I am now quite contented and am very much
occupied in reviewing the Junior studies, as I wish to enter
the middle class. The school is very large, and though quite a
number have left, on account of finding the examinations
more difficult than they anticipated, yet there are nearly 300
now. Perhaps you know that Miss Lyon is raising her stan-
dard of scholarship a good deal, on account of the number of
applicants this year, and she makes the examinations more
severe than usual.

You cannot imagine how trying they are, because if we

cannot go through them all in a specified time, we are sent home. I cannot be too thankful that I got through as soon as I did, and I am sure that I never would endure the suspense which I endured during those three days again for all the treasures of the world.

I room with my cousin Emily, who is a Senior. She is an excellent room-mate, and does all in her power to make me happy. You can imagine how pleasant a good room-mate is, for you have been away to school so much. Everything is pleasant and happy here, and I think I could be no happier at any other school away from home. Things seem much more like home than I anticipated, and the teachers are all very kind and affectionate to us. They call on us frequently and urge us to return their calls, and when we do, we always receive a cordial welcome from them.

I will tell you my order of time for the day, as you were so kind as to give me yours. At 6 o'clock we all rise. We breakfast at 7. Our study hours begin at 8. At 9 we all meet in Seminary Hall for devotions. At 10¼ I recite a review of Ancient History, in connection with which we read Goldsmith and Grimshaw. At 11, I recite a lesson in Pope's *Essay on Man*, which is merely transposition. At 12 I practice calisthenics, and at 12¼ read until dinner, which is at 12½, and after dinner, from 1½ until 2, I sing in Seminary Hall. From 2¾ until 3¾ I practise upon the piano. At 3¾ I go to Sections, where we give in all our accounts for the day, including absence, tardiness, communications, breaking silent study hours, receiving company in our rooms, and ten thousand other things which I will not take time or place to mention. At 4½ we go into Seminary Hall and receive advice from Miss Lyon in the form of a lecture. We have supper at 6, and study silent hours from then until the retiring bell, which rings at 8¾, but the tardy bell does not ring until 9¾, so that we don't often obey the first warning to retire. Unless we have a good and reasonable excuse for failure upon any of the items that I mentioned above, they are recorded and a *black mark* stands against our names. As you can easily imagine, we do not like very well to get "exceptions," as they are called scientifically here.

My domestic work is not difficult and consists in carrying the knives from the first tier of tables at morning and noon, and at night washing and wiping the same quantity of knives. I am quite well and hope to spend the year here, free from sickness.

You have probably heard many reports of the food here; and if so, I can tell you that I have yet seen nothing corresponding to my ideas on that point from what I have heard. Everything is wholesome and abundant and much nicer than I should imagine could be provided for almost 300 girls. We have also a great variety upon our tables and frequent changes. One thing is certain, and that is, that Miss Lyon and all the teachers seem to consult our comfort and happiness in everything they do, and you know that is pleasant. When I left home I did not think I should find a companion or a dear friend in all the multitude. I expected to find rough and uncultivated manners, and, to be sure, I have found some of that stamp, but on the whole, there is an ease and grace, a desire to make one another happy, which delights and at the same time surprises me very much. I find no Abby nor Abiah nor Mary, but I love many of the girls. Austin came to see me when I had been here about two weeks, and brought Viny and A. I need not tell you how delighted I was to see them all, nor how happy it made me to hear them say that "they were *so lonely.*" It is a sweet feeling to know that you are missed and that your memory is precious at home. This week, on Wednesday, I was at my window, when I happened to look towards the hotel and saw father and mother, walking over here as dignified as you please. I need not tell you that I danced and clapped my hands, and flew to meet them, for you can imagine how I felt. I will only ask you, do you love your parents? They wanted to surprise me, and for that reason did not let me know they were coming. I could not bear to have them go, but go they must, and so I submitted in sadness. Only to think that in 2¹/₂ weeks I shall be at my *own dear home* again. You will probably go home at Thanksgiving time, and we can rejoice with each other.

You don't [know] how I laughed at your description of your introduction to Daniel Webster, and I read that part of your letter to cousin Emily. You must feel quite proud of the acquaintance, and will not, I hope, be vain in consequence. However, you don't know Governor Briggs, and I do, so you are no better off than I. . . . A., you must write me often, and I shall write you as often as I have time. . . .

From your affectionate
Emily E. D.

To Abiah Root

Mt. Holyoke Female Seminary, Jan. 17, 1848

My Dear Abiah,—Your welcome epistle found me upon the eve of going home, and it is needless to say very happy. We all went home on Wednesday before Thanksgiving, and a stormy day it was, but the storm must not be in our way, so we tried to make the best of it and look as cheerful as we could. Many of the girls went very early in the morning in order to reach home the same day, and when we all sat down to the breakfast table, it seemed lonely enough to see so many places vacant. After breakfast, as we were not required to keep all the family rules, a number of us met together at one of the windows in the Hall to watch for our friends, whom we were constantly expecting. No morning of my life ever passed so slowly to me, and it really seemed to me they never were coming, so impatiently did I await their arrival. At last, almost tired out, I spied a carriage in the distance, and surely Austin was in it. You, who have been away so much, can easily imagine my delight and will not laugh, when I tell you how I dashed downstairs and almost frightened my dignified brother out of his senses. All was ready in a moment or less than a moment, and cousin Emily and myself, not forgetting the driver, were far on our way toward home. The rain fell in torrents and the wind howled around the sides of the mountain over our heads, and the brooks below, filled by the rain, rushed along their pebbly beds almost frightfully, yet nothing daunted, we rode swiftly along, and soon the colleges and the spire of our venerable meeting-house rose to my delighted vision.

Never did Amherst look more lovely to me, and gratitude rose in my heart to God, for granting me such a safe return to my *own dear home*. Soon the carriage stopped in front of our own house, and all were at the door to welcome the returned one, from mother, with tears in her eyes, down to pussy, who tried to look as gracious as was becoming to her dignity. Oh, Abiah, it was the first meeting, as it had been the first separation, and it was a joyful one to all of us.

The storm did not subside that night, but in the morning I was waked by the glorious sunshine staring full in my face. We went to church in the morning and listened to an excellent sermon from our own minister, Mr. Colton. At noon we returned and had a nice dinner, which, you well know, cannot be dispensed with on Thanksgiving day. We had several calls in the afternoon, and had four invitations out for the evening. Of course we could not accept them all, much to my sorrow, but decided to make two visits. At about 7 o'clock father, mother, Austin, Viny, cousin Emily, and my-self to bring up at the rear, went to Professor Warner's, where we spent an hour delightfully with a few friends, and then bidding them good eve, we young folks went down to Mrs. S. Mack's, accompanied by *sister Mary*. There was quite a company of young people assembled when we arrived, and after we had played many games we had, in famil-iar terms, a "candy scrape." We enjoyed the evening much, and returned not until the clock pealed out, "Remember ten o'clock, my dear, remember ten o'clock." After our return, father wishing to hear the piano, I, like an obedient daugh-ter, played and sang a few tunes, much to his apparent gratification. We then retired, and the next day and the next were as happily spent as the eventful Thanksgiving day itself.

You will probably think me foolish thus to give you an inventory of my time while at home, but I did enjoy so much in those short four days that I wanted you to know and enjoy it too. Monday came so soon, and with it came a carriage to our door, and amidst tears falling thick and fast away I went again. Slowly and sadly dragged a few of the days after my return to the Seminary, and I was very homesick, but "after a storm there comes a calm," and so it was in my case. My sorrows were soon lost in study, and I again felt happy, if happiness there can be away from "home, sweet home."

Our term closes this week on Thursday, and Friday I hope to see home and friends once more. I have studied hard this term, and aside from my delight at going home, there is a sweetness in approaching rest to me. This term is the longest in the year, and I would not wish to live it over again, I can assure you. I love this Seminary, and all the teachers are bound strongly to my heart by ties of affection. There are many sweet girls here, and dearly do I love some new faces, but I have not yet found the place of a *few* dear ones filled, nor would I wish it to be here. I am now studying Silliman's Chemistry and Cutter's Physiology, in both of which I am much interested. We finish Physiology before this term closes, and are to be examined in it at the spring examinations, about five weeks after the commencement of the next term. I already begin to dread that time, for an examination in Mount Holyoke Seminary is rather more public than in our old academy, and a failure would be more disgraceful then, I opine; but I hope, to use my father's own words, "that I shall not disgrace myself." What are you studying now? You did not mention that item in your last letters to me, and consequently I am quite in the dark as regards your progress in those affairs. All I can say is, that I hope you will not leave poor me far behind. . . .

Your affectionate *sister*
Emily E. Dickinson

To her brother Austin
[South Hadley, about Feb. 14, 1848]

My dear Austin,—You will perhaps imagine from my date that I am quite at leisure, and can do what I please even in the forenoon, but one of our teachers, who is engaged, received a visit from her intended quite unexpectedly yesterday afternoon, and she has gone to her home to show him, I opine, and will be absent until Saturday. As I happen to recite to her in one of my studies, her absence gives me a little time in which to write.

Your welcome letter found me all engrossed in the study of sulphuric acid! I deliberated for a few moments after its reception on the propriety of carrying it to Miss Whitman, your friend. The result of my deliberation was a conclusion to open it with moderation, peruse its contents with sobriety becoming my station, and if after a close investigation of its contents I found nothing which savored of rebellion or an unsubdued will, I would lay it away in my folio, and forget I had received it. Are you not gratified that I am so rapidly gaining correct ideas of female propriety and sedate deportment? After the proposed examination, finding it concealed no dangerous sentiments, I with great gravity deposited it with my other letters, and the impression that I once had such a letter is entirely obliterated by the waves of time.

I have been quite lonely since I came back, but cheered by the thought that I am not to return another year, I take comfort, and still hope on. My visit at home was happy, very happy to me; and had the idea of in so short a time returning been constantly in my dreams by night and day, I could not have been happier. "There is no rose without a thorn" to me. Home was always dear to me, and dearer still the friends around it; but never did it seem so dear as now. All, all are kind to me, but their tones fall strangely on my ear, and their countenances meet mine not like home-faces, I can assure you most sincerely. Then when tempted to feel sad, I think of the blazing fire and the cheerful meal and the chair empty now I am gone. I can hear the cheerful voices and the merry laugh, and a desolate feeling comes home to my heart, to think I am alone. But my good angel only waits to see the tears coming and then whispers, "Only this year! only twenty-two weeks more, and then home again you will be to stay." To you, all busy and excited, I suppose the time flies faster; but to me slowly, very slowly, so that I can see his chariot wheels when they roll along, and himself is often visible. But I will no longer imagine, for your brain is full of *Arabian Nights'* fancies, and it will not do to pour fuel on your already kindled imagination. . . .

I suppose you have written a few and received a quantity of valentines this week. Every night have I looked, and yet in vain, for one of Cupid's messengers. Many of the girls have received very beautiful ones; and I have not quite done hoping for one. Surely my friend *Thomas* has not lost all his former affection for me! I entreat you to tell him I am pining for a valentine. I am sure I shall not very soon forget last Valentine week, nor any the sooner the fun I had at that time. . . . Monday afternoon Mistress Lyon arose in the hall, and forbade our sending "any of those foolish notes called valentines." But those who were here last year, knowing her opinions, were sufficiently cunning to write and give them into the care of D. during the vacation; so that about 150 were despatched on Valentine morn, before orders should be put down to the contrary effect. Hearing of this act, Miss Whitman, by and with the advice and consent of the other teachers, with frowning brow, sallied over to the Post Office to ascertain, if possible, the number of the valentines, and worse still, the names of the offenders. Nothing has yet been heard as to the amount of her information, but as D. is a good hand to help the girls, and no one has yet received sentence, we begin to think her mission unsuccessful. I have not written one, nor do I intend to. . . .

Your affectionate sister
Emily

To Abiah Root

Mount Holyoke Female Seminary
May 16, 1848

My dear Abiah,—You must forgive me, indeed you must, that I have so long delayed to write you, and I doubt not you will when I give you all my reasons for so doing. You know it is customary for the first page to be occupied with apologies, and I must not depart from the beaten track for one of my own imagining. . . . I had not been very well all winter, but had not written home about it, lest the folks should take me home. During the week following examinations, a friend from Amherst came over and spent a week with me, and when that friend returned home, father and mother were duly notified of the state of my health. Have you so treacherous a friend?

Not knowing that I was to be reported at home, you can imagine my amazement and consternation when Saturday of the same week Austin arrived in full sail, with orders from head-quarters to bring me home at all events. At first I had recourse to words, and a desperate battle with those weapons was waged for a few moments, between my *Sophomore* brother and myself. Finding words of no avail, I next resorted to tears. But woman's tears are of little avail, and I am sure mine flowed in vain. As you can imagine, Austin was victorious, and poor, defeated I was led off in triumph. You must not imbibe the idea from what I have said that I do not love home—far from it. But I could not bear to leave teachers and companions before the close of the term and go home to be dosed and receive the physician daily, and take warm drinks and be condoled with on the state of health in general by all the old ladies in town.

Haven't I given a ludicrous account of going home sick from a boarding-school? Father is quite a hand to give medicine, especially if it is not desirable to the patient, and I was dosed for about a month after my return home, without any mercy, till at last out of mere pity my cough went away, and I had quite a season of peace. Thus I remained at home until the close of the term, comforting my parents by my presence, and instilling many a lesson of wisdom into the budding intellect of my only sister. I had almost forgotten to tell you that I went on with my studies at home, and kept up with my class. Last Thursday our vacation closed, and on Friday morn, midst the weeping of friends, crowing of roosters, and singing of birds, I again took my departure from home. Five days have now passed since we returned to Holyoke, and they have passed very slowly. Thoughts of home and friends "come crowding thick and fast, like lightnings from the mountain cloud," and it seems very desolate.

Father has decided not to send me to Holyoke another year, so this is my *last term*. Can it be possible that I have been here almost a year? It startles me when I really think of the advantages I have had, and I fear I have not improved them as I ought. But many an hour has fled with its report to heaven, and what has been the tale of me? . . . How glad I am that spring has come, and how it calms my mind when wearied with study to walk out in the green fields and beside the pleasant streams in which South Hadley is rich! There are not many wild flowers near, for the girls have driven them to a distance, and we are obliged to walk quite a distance to find them, but they repay us by their sweet smiles and fragrance.

The older I grow, the more do I love spring and spring flowers. Is it so with you? While at home there were several pleasure parties of which I was a member, and in our rambles we found many and beautiful children of spring, which I will mention and see if you have found them,—the trailing arbutus, adder's tongue, yellow violets, liver-leaf, blood-root, and many other smaller flowers.

What are you reading now? I have little time to read when I am here, but while at home I had a feast in the reading line, I can assure you. Two or three of them I will mention: "Evangeline," "The Princess," "The Maiden Aunt," "The Epicurean," and "The Twins and Heart," by Tupper, complete the list. Am not I a pedant for telling you what I have been reading? Have you forgotten your visit at Amherst last summer, and what delightful times we had? I have not, and I hope you will come and make another and a longer, when I get home from Holyoke. Father wishes to have me at home a year, and he will probably send me away again, where I know not.

Ever your own affectionate
Emilie E. Dickinson

To Abiah Root

Amherst, Jan. 29, 1850

Very dear Abiah,—The folks have all gone away; they thought that they left me alone, and contrived things to amuse me should they stay long, and *I* be lonely. Lonely, indeed,—they didn't look, and they couldn't have seen if they had, who should bear me company. *Three* here, instead of *one*, wouldn't it scare them? A curious trio, part earthly and part spiritual two of us, the other, all heaven, and no earth. *God* is sitting here, looking into my very soul to see if I think right thoughts. Yet I am not afraid, for I try to be right and good; and He knows every one of my struggles. He looks very gloriously, and everything bright seems dull beside Him; and I don't dare to look directly at Him for fear I shall die. Then *you* are here, dressed in that quiet black gown and cap,—that funny little cap I used to laugh at you about,—and you don't appear to be thinking about anything in particular,—not in one of your *breaking-dish* moods, I take it. You seem aware that I'm writing you, and are amused, I should think, at any such friendly manifestation when you are already present. *Success,* however, even in making a fool of myself, isn't to be despised; so I shall persist in writing, and you may in laughing at me,—if you are fully aware of the value of time as regards your immortal spirit. I can't say that I advise you to laugh; but if you are punished, and I warned you, that can be no business of mine. So I fold up my arms, and leave you to fate—may it deal very kindly with you! The trinity winds up with me, as you may have surmised, and I certainly wouldn't be at the fag-end but for civility to you. This self-sacrificing spirit will be the ruin of me!

I am occupied principally with a cold just now, and the dear creature *will* have so much attention that my time slips away amazingly. It has heard *so* much of New Englanders, of their kind attentions to strangers, that it's come all the way from the Alps to determine the truth of the tale. It says the half wasn't told it, and I begin to be afraid it wasn't. Only think—came all the way from that distant Switzerland to find what was the truth! Neither husband, protector, nor friend accompanied it, and so utter a state of loneliness gives friends if nothing else. You are dying of curiosity; let me arrange that pillow to make your exit easier. I stayed at home all Saturday afternoon, and treated some disagreeable people who insisted upon calling here as tolerably as I could; when evening shades began to fall, I turned upon my heel, and walked. Attracted by the gayety visible in the street, I still kept walking till a little creature pounced upon a thin shawl I wore, and commenced riding. I stopped, and begged the creature to alight, as I was fatigued already, and quite unable to assist others. It wouldn't get down, and commenced talking to itself: "Can't be New England—must have made some mistake—disappointed in my reception— don't agree with accounts. Oh, what a world of deception and fraud! Marm, will you tell me the name of this country —it's Asia Minor, isn't it? I intended to stop in New England." By this time I was so completely exhausted that I made no further effort to rid me of my load, and travelled home at a moderate jog, paying no attention whatever to it, got into the house, threw off both bonnet and shawl, and out flew my tormentor, and putting both arms around my neck, began to kiss me immoderately, and express so much love it completely bewildered me. Since then it has slept in my bed, eaten from my plate, lived with me everywhere, and will tag me through life for all I know. I think I'll wake first, and get out of bed, and leave it; but early or late, it is dressed before me, and sits on the side of the bed looking right into my face with such a comical expression it almost makes me laugh in spite of myself. I can't call it interesting, but it certainly *is* curious, has two peculiarities which would quite win your heart,—a huge pocket-handkerchief and a very red nose. The first seems so very *abundant,* it gives you the idea of independence and prosperity in business. The last brings up the "jovial bowl, my boys," and such an association's worth the having. If it *ever* gets tired of *me,* I will forward it to *you*—you would love it for *my* sake, if not for its own; it will tell you some queer stories about me,—how I sneezed so loud one night that the family thought the last trump was sounding, and climbed into the currant-bushes to get out of the way; how the rest of the people, arrayed in long night-gowns, folded their arms, and were waiting; but this is a wicked story,—it can tell some better ones. Now, my dear friend, let me tell you that these last thoughts are fictions,—vain imaginations to lead astray foolish young women. They are flowers of speech; they both make and tell deliberate falsehoods; avoid them as the snake, and turn aside as from the rattle-snake, and I don't *think* you will be harmed. Honestly, though, a snake-bite is a serious matter, and there can't be too much said or done about it. The big serpent bites the deepest; and we get so accustomed to its bites that we don't mind about them. "Verily I say unto you, fear *him."* Won't you read some work upon snakes?—I have a real anxiety for you. *I* love those little green ones that slide around by your shoes in the grass, and make it rustle with their elbows; they are rather my favorites on the whole; but I wouldn't influence *you* for the world. There is an air of misanthropy about the striped snake that will commend itself at once to your taste,—there is no monotony about it—but we will more of this again. Something besides severe colds and serpents, and we will try to find *that* something. It can't be a garden, can it? or a strawberry-bed, which rather belongs to a garden; nor it can't be a school-house, nor an attorney-at-law. Oh, dear! I don't know what it is. Love for the absent don't *sound* like it; but try it and see how it goes.

I miss you very much indeed; think of you at night when the world's nodding, nid, nid, nodding—think of you in the daytime when the cares of the world, and its continual vexations choke up the love for friends in some of our hearts; remember your warnings sometimes—try to do as you told me sometimes—and sometimes conclude it's no use to try; then my heart says it *is,* and new trial is followed by disappointment again. I wondered, when you had gone, why we didn't talk more,—it wasn't for want of a subject; it never *could be* for *that.* Too many, perhaps,—such a crowd of people that nobody heard the speaker, and all went away discontented. You astonished me in the outset, perplexed me in the continuance, and wound up in a grand snarl I shall be all my pilgrimage unravelling. Rather a dismal prospect certainly; but "it's always the darkest the hour before day," and this earlier sunset promises an earlier rise—a sun in splendor—and glory, flying out of its purple nest. Wouldn't you love to see God's bird, when it first tries its wings? If you were here I would tell you something—several somethings—which have happened since you went away; but time and space, as usual, oppose themselves, and I put my treasures away till "we two meet again." The hope that I shall continue in love towards you, and *vice versa,* will sustain me till then. If you are thinking soon to go away, and to show your face no more, just inform me, will you? I would have the "long, lingering look," which you cast behind,—it would be an invaluable addition to my treasures, and "keep your memory green." "Lord, keep all our memories green," and help on our affection, and tie the "link that doth us bind" in a tight bow-knot that will keep it from separation, and stop us from growing old; if that is impossible, make old age pleasant to us, put its arms around us kindly, and when we go home, let that home be called Heaven.

Your very sincere and wicked friend
Emily E. Dickinson

To Abiah Root

Dear Remembered,—The circumstances under which I write you this morning are at once glorious, afflicting, and beneficial,—glorious in *ends,* afflicting in *means,* and beneficial, I trust, in *both.* Twin loaves of bread have just been born into the world under my auspices,—fine children, the image of their mother; and here, my dear friend, is the *glory.*

On the lounge, asleep, lies my sick mother, suffering intensely from acute neuralgia, except at a moment like this, when kind sleep draws near, and beguiles her,—here is the *affliction.*

I need not draw the beneficial inference,—the good I myself derive, the winning the spirit of patience, the genial housekeeping influence stealing over my mind and soul,—you know all these things I would say, and will seem to suppose they are written, when indeed they are only thought.

On Sunday my mother was taken, had been perfectly well before, and could remember no possible imprudence which should have induced the disease. Everything has been done, and though we think her gradually throwing it off, she still has much suffering. I have always neglected the culinary arts, but attend to them now from necessity, and from a desire to make everything pleasant for father and Austin. Sickness makes desolation, and the day is dark and dreary; but health will come back, I hope, and light hearts and smiling faces. We are sick hardly ever at home, and don't know what to do when it comes,—wrinkle our little brows, and stamp with our little feet, and our tiny souls get angry, and command it to go away. Mrs. Brown will be glad to see it,—old ladies expect to die; "as for *us,* the young and active, with all longings 'for the strife,' *we* to perish by the roadside, weary with the 'march of life'—no, no, my dear 'Father Mortality,' get out of the way if you please; we will call if we ever want you. Good-morning, sir! ah, good-morning!"

When I am not at work, I sit by the side of mother, provide for her little wants, and try to cheer and encourage her. I ought to be glad and grateful that I *can* do anything now, but I do feel so very lonely, and so anxious to have her cured. I haven't repined but once, and you shall know all the why. At noon . . . I heard a well-known rap, and a friend I love *so* dearly came and asked me to ride in the woods, the sweet, still woods,—and I wanted to exceedingly. I told him I could not go, and he said he was disappointed, he wanted me very much. Then the tears came into my eyes, though I tried to choke them back, and he said I *could* and *should* go, and it seemed to me unjust. Oh, I struggled with great temptation, and it cost me much of denial; but I think in the end I conquered,—not a glorious victory, where you hear the rolling drum, but a kind of a helpless victory, where triumph would come of itself, faintest music, weary soldiers, nor a waving flag, nor a long, loud shout. I had read of Christ's temptations, and how they were like our own, only he didn't sin; I wondered if *one* was like mine, and whether it made him angry. I couldn't make up my mind; do you think he ever did?

I went cheerfully round my work, humming a little air till mother had gone to sleep, then cried with all my might— seemed to think I was much abused—that this wicked world was unworthy such devoted and terrible suffering—and came to my various senses in great dudgeon at life, and time, and love for affliction and anguish.

What shall we do, my darling, when trial grows more and more, when the dim, lone light expires, and it's dark, so very dark, and we wander, and know not where, and cannot get out of the forest—whose is the hand to help us, and to lead, and forever guide us; they talk of a "Jesus of Nazareth"— will you tell me if it be he? . . .

It's Friday, my dear A., and that in another week, yet my mission is unfulfilled—and you so sadly neglected, and don't know the reason why. Where do you think I've strayed, and from what new errand returned? I have come from "to

and fro, and walking up and down" the same place that
Satan hailed from, when God asked him where he'd been;
but not to illustrate further, I tell you I have been dreaming,
dreaming a *golden* dream, with eyes all the while wide
open, and I guess it's almost morning; and besides, I have
been at work, providing the "food that perisheth," scaring
the timorous dust, and being obedient and kind. I am yet the
Queen of the Court, if regalia be dust and dirt, have three
loyal subjects, whom I'd rather relieve from service. Mother
is still an invalid, though a partially restored one; father
and Austin still clamor for food; and I, like a martyr, am
feeding them. Wouldn't you love to see me in these bonds
of great despair, looking around my kitchen, and praying
for kind deliverance, and declaring by "Omai's beard"
I never was in such plight? *My* kitchen, I think I called
it—God forbid that it was, or shall be, my own—God keep
me from what they call *households,* except that bright one
of "faith"!

Don't be afraid of my imprecations—they never did any
one harm, and they make me feel so cool, and so very much
more comfortable! . . . I presume you are loving your
mother, and loving the stranger and wanderer—visiting the
poor and afflicted, and reaping whole fields of blessings—
save me a little sheaf, only a very little one! Remember and
care for me sometimes, and scatter a fragrant flower in this
wilderness life of mine by writing me, and by not forgetting,
and by lingering longer in prayer, that the Father may bless
one more!

Your affectionate friend
Emily

To Elbridge G. Bowdoin

Valentine Week [1850]

Awake, ye muses nine, sing me a strain divine,
Unwind the solemn twine, and tie my Valentine.

Oh the earth was *made* for lovers, for damsel, and
    hopeless swain,
For sighing, and gentle whispering, and *unity* made of
    twain.
All things do go a courting, in earth or sea, or air,
God hath made nothing single but *thee* in His world so
    fair!
The *bride* and then the *bridegroom,* the *two,* and then the
    one,
Adam, and Eve, his consort, the moon and then the sun;
The life doth prove the precept, who obey shall happy be,
Who will not serve the sovereign, be hanged on fatal tree.
The high do seek the lowly, the great do seek the small,
None cannot find who seeketh, on this terrestrial ball;
The bee doth court the flower, the flower his suit receives,
And they make a merry wedding, whose guests are
    hundred leaves;
The wind doth woo the branches, the branches they are
    won,
And the father fond demandeth the maiden for his son.
The storm doth walk the seashore humming a mournful
    tune,
The wave with eye so pensive looketh to see the moon,
Their spirits meet together, they make them solemn vows,
No more he singeth mournful, her sadness she doth lose.
The worm doth woo the mortal, death claims a living
    bride,
Night unto day is married, morn unto eventide;
Earth is a merry damsel, and heaven a knight so true,
And Earth is quite coquettish, and beseemeth in vain to
    sue.
Now to the application, to the reading of the roll,
To bringing thee to justice, and marshalling thy soul:
Thou art a *human* solo, a being cold, and lone,
Wilt have no kind companion, thou reapest what thou hast
    sown.
Hast never silent hours, and minutes all too long,
And a deal of sad reflection, and wailing instead of song?
There's *Sarah,* and *Eliza,* and *Emeline* so fair,

And *Harriet* and *Sabra,* and she with curling hair.
Thine eyes are sadly blinded, but yet thou mayest see
Six true and comely maidens sitting upon the tree;
Approach that tree with caution, then up it boldly climb,
And seize the one thou lovest, nor care for space, or time.
Then bear her to the greenwood, and build for her a
    bower,
And give her what she asketh, jewel, or bird, or flower—
And bring the fife, and trumpet, and beat upon the drum—
And bid the world Goodmorrow, and go to glory home!

To Abiah Root
[January, 1851]

I write Abiah tonight, because it is cool and quiet, and I can
forget the toil and care of the feverish day, and then I am
selfish too, because I am feeling lonely; some of my friends
are gone, and some of my friends are sleeping—sleeping the
churchyard sleep—the hour of evening is sad—it was once
my study hour—my master has gone to rest, and the open
leaf of the book, and the scholar at school *alone,* make the
tears come, and I cannot brush them away; I would not if I
could, for they are the only tribute I can pay the departed
Humphrey.

You have stood by the grave before; I have walked there
sweet summer evenings and read the names on the stones,
and wondered who would come and give me the same me-
morial; but I never have laid my friends there, and forgot
that they too must die; this is my first affliction, and indeed
'tis hard to bear it. To those bereaved so often that home is
no more here, and whose communion with friends is had
only in prayers, there must be much to hope for, but when
the unreconciled spirit has nothing left but God, that spirit is
lone indeed. I don't think there will be any sunshine, or any
singing birds in the spring that's coming. . . . I will try not
to say anything more—my rebellious thoughts are many, and
the friend I love and trust in has much *now* to forgive. I wish

I were somebody else—I would pray the prayer of the "Pharisee," but I am a poor little "Publican." "Son of David," look down on me!

'Twas a great while ago when you wrote me, I remember the leaves were falling—and *now* there are falling snows; who maketh the two to differ—are not leaves the brethren of snows?

Then it *can't* be a great while since then, though I verily thought it *was*; we are not so young as we once were, and time seems to be growing long. I dream of being a grandame, and banding my silver hairs, and I seem to be quite submissive to the thought of growing old; no doubt you ride rocking-horses in your present as in young sleeps—quite a pretty contrast indeed, of me braiding my own gray hairs, and my friend at play with her childhood, a pair of decayed old ladies! Where *are* you, my *antique* friend, or my very dear and young one—just as you please to please—it *may* seem quite a presumption that I address you at all, knowing not if you habit here, or if my "bird has flown" in which world her wing is folded. When I think of the friends I love, and the little while we may dwell here, and then "we go away," I have a yearning feeling, a desire eager and anxious lest any be stolen away, so that I cannot behold them. I would have you here, all here, where I can *see* you, and *hear* you, and where I can say "Oh, no," if the "Son of Man" ever "cometh"!

It is not enough, now and then, at long and uncertain intervals to hear you're alive and well. I do not care for the body, I love the timid soul, the blushing, shrinking soul; it hides, for it is afraid, and the bold, obtrusive body—Pray, marm, did you call *me*? We are very small, Abiah—I think we grow still smaller—this tiny insect life the portal to another; it seems strange—strange indeed. I'm afraid we are all unworthy, yet we shall "enter in."

I can think of no other way than for you, my dear girl, to come here—we are growing away from each other, and talk even now like strangers. To forget the "meum and teum," *dearest* friends must meet sometimes, and then comes the "bond of the spirit" which, if I am correct, is "unity."

You are growing wiser than I am, and nipping in the bud fancies which I let blossom—perchance to bear no fruit, or if plucked, I may find it bitter. The shore is safer, Abiah, but I love to buffet the sea—I can count the bitter wrecks here in these pleasant waters, and hear the murmuring winds, but oh, I love the danger! You are learning control and firmness. Christ Jesus will love you more. I'm afraid he don't love me *any!* . . . Write when you *will,* my friend, and forget all amiss herein, for as these few imperfect words to the full communion of spirits, so this small giddy life to the *better,* the life eternal, and that *we* may live this life, and be filled with this true communion, I shall not cease to pray.

E.

To *her brother Austin*
[Amherst, 1851]

. . . We are enjoying this evening what is called a "northeast storm"—a little north of east in case you are pretty definite. Father thinks it's "amazin' raw," and I'm half disposed to think that he's in the right about it, though I keep pretty dark and don't say much about it! Vinnie is at the instrument, humming a pensive air concerning a young lady who thought she was "almost there." Vinnie seems much grieved, and I really suppose *I* ought to betake myself to weeping; I'm pretty sure that I *shall* if she don't abate her singing.

Father's just got home from meeting and Mr. Boltwood's, found the last quite comfortable and the first not quite so well. . . . There has been not much stirring since when you went away—I should venture to say prudently that matters had come to a stand—unless something new "turns up," I cannot see anything to prevent a quiet season. Father takes care of the doors and mother of the windows, and Vinnie and I are secure against all outward attacks. If we can get our hearts "under," I don't have much to fear—

I've got all but three feelings down, if I can only keep them! . . .

I shall think of you to-morrow with four and twenty Irish boys all in a row. I miss you very much—I put on my bonnet to-night, opened the gate very desperately, and for a little while the suspense was terrible—I think I was held in check by some invisible agent, for I returned to the house without having done any harm!

If I hadn't been afraid that you would "poke fun" at my feelings, I had written a sincere letter, but since "the world is hollow, and dollie's stuffed with sawdust," I really do not think we had better expose our feelings. . . .

Your dear sister

Emily

To her brother Austin
[July 5, 1851]

I have just come in from church very hot and faded. . . . Our church grows interesting—Zion lifts her head—I over-hear remarks signifying Jerusalem,—I do not feel at liberty to say any more to-day!

. . . I wanted to write you Friday, the night of Jennie Lind, but reaching home past midnight, and my room some-time after, encountering several perils starting and on the way, among which a kicking horse, an inexperienced driver, a number of Jove's thunderbolts, and a very terrible rain, are worthy to have record. All of us went—just four—add an absent individual and that will make full five. The concert commenced at eight, but knowing the world was *hollow* we thought we'd start at six, and come up with everybody that meant to come up with us; we had proceeded some steps when one of the beasts showed symptoms; and just by the blacksmith's shop exercises commenced, consisting of kick-ing and plunging on the part of the horse, and whips and moral suasion from the gentleman who drove—the horse re-fused to proceed, and your respected family with much chagrin dismounted, advanced to the hotel, and for a season halted; another horse procured, we were politely invited to take our seats, and proceed, which we refused to do till the animal was warranted. About half through our journey thunder was said to be heard, and a suspicious cloud came travelling up the sky. What words express our horror when rain began to fall, in drops, sheets, cataracts—what fancy conceive of drippings and of drenchings which we met on the way; how the stage and its mourning captives drew up at Warner's Hotel; how all of us alighted, and were conducted in,—how the rain did not abate,—how we walked in silence to the old Edwards church and took our seats in the same—how Jennie came out like a child and sang and sang again—how bouquets fell in showers, and the roof was rent with applause—how it thundered outside, and inside with the thunder of God and of men—judge ye which was the loudest; how we all loved Jennie Lind, but not accustomed oft to her manner of singing didn't fancy *that* so well as we did *her.* No doubt it was very fine, but take some notes from her *Echo,* the bird sounds from the *Bird Song,* and some of her curious trills, and I'd rather have a Yankee.

Herself and not her music was what we seemed to love— she has an air of exile in her mild blue eyes, and a something sweet and touching in her native accent which charms her many friends. *Give me my thatched cottage* as she sang she grew so earnest she seemed half lost in song, and for a transient time I fancied she *had* found it and would be seen "na mair"; and then her foreign accent made her again a wanderer—we will talk about her sometime when you come. Father sat all the evening looking *mad,* and yet so much amused you would have *died* a-laughing. . . . It wasn't sarcasm exactly, nor it wasn't disdain, it was infinitely funnier than either of those virtues, as if old Abraham had come to see the show, and thought it was all very well, but a little excess of *monkey!* She took $4,000 for tickets at Northampton aside from all expenses. . . .

About our coming to Boston—we think we shall probably come—we want to see our friends, yourself and Aunt L.'s family. We don't care a fig for the Museum, the stillness, or Jennie Lind. . . . Love from us all.

Your affectionate sister

Emily

To her brother Austin

[August, 1851]

At my old stand again, dear Austin, and happy as a queen to know that while I speak those whom I love are listening, and I am happier still if I shall make them happy.

I have just finished reading your letter which was brought in since church. I like it grandly—very—because it is so long, and also it's *so* funny—we have all been laughing till the old house rung again at your delineation of men, women, and things. I feel quite like retiring in presence of one so grand, and casting my small lot among small birds and fishes; you say you don't comprehend me, you want a simpler style— gratitude indeed for all my fine philosophy! I strove to be exalted, thinking I might reach *you*, and while I pant and struggle and climb the nearest cloud, you walk out very leisurely in your slippers from Empyrean, and without the slightest notice, request me to get down! As simple as you please, the simplest sort of simple—I'll be a little ninny, a little pussy catty, a little Red Riding Hood; I'll wear a bee in my bonnet, and a rose-bud in my hair, and what remains to do you shall be told hereafter.

Your letters are richest treats, send them always just such warm days—they are worth a score of fans and many refrigerators—the only difficulty they are so *queer*, and laughing such hot weather is anything but amusing. A little more of earnest, and a little less of jest until we are out of August, and then you may joke as freely as the father of rogues himself, and we will banish care, and daily die a-laughing!

It is very hot here now; I don't believe it's any hotter in

Boston than it is here. . . . Vinnie suggests that she may sometimes occur to mind when you would like more collars made. I told her I wouldn't tell you—I haven't, however, decided whether I will or not.

I often put on five knives and forks, and another tumbler, forgetting for the moment that "we are not all here." It occurs to me, however, and I remove the extra, and brush a tear away in memory of my brother.

We miss you now and always. When God bestows but three, and one of those is withdrawn, the others are left alone. . . . Father is as uneasy when you are gone away as if you catch a trout and put him in Sahara. When you first went away he came home very frequently—walked gravely towards the barn, and returned looking very stately—then strode away down street as if the foe was coming; *now* he is more resigned—contents himself by fancying that "we shall hear to-day," and then when we do not hear, he wags his head profound, and thinks without a doubt there will be news "to-morrow." "Once one is two," once one will be two —ah, I have it here!

I wish you could have some cherries—if there was any way we would send you a basket of them—they are very large and delicious, and are just ripening now. Little Austin Grout comes every day to pick them, and mother takes great comfort in calling him by name, from vague association with her departed boy. Austin, to tell the truth, it is very still and lonely—I do wish you were here. . . . The railroad is "a-workin'." My love to all my friends. I am on my way downstairs to put the tea-kettle boiling—writing and taking tea cannot sympathize. If you forget me now, your right hand *shall* its cunning.

Emilie

To her brother Austin
[Amherst, July, 1851]

. . . You'd better not come home; I say the law will have you, a pupil of the law o'ertaken by the law, and brought to condign punishment,—scene for angels and men, or rather for archangels, who being a little higher would seem to have a 'vantage so far as view's concerned. *"Are* you pretty comfortable, though,"—and are you deaf and dumb and gone to the asylum where such afflicted persons learn to hold their tongues?

The next time you aren't going to write me, I'd thank you to let me know—this kind of *protracted* insult is what no man can bear. Fight with me like a man—let me have fair shot, and you are *caput mortuum et cap-a-pie,* and that ends the business! If you really think I so deserve this silence, tell me why—how—I'll be a thorough scamp or else I won't be any, just which you prefer. . . .

Yesterday there was a fire. At about three in the afternoon Mr. Kimberly's barn was discovered to be on fire; the wind was blowing a gale directly from the west, and having had no rain, the roofs [were] as dry as stubble. Mr. Palmer's house was charred—the little house of father's—and Mr. Kimberly's also. The engine was broken, and it seemed for a little while as if the whole street must go; the Kimberlys' barn was burnt down, and the house much charred and injured, though not at all destroyed—Mr. Palmer's barn took fire, and Deacon Leland's also, but were extinguished with only part burned roofs. We all feel very thankful at such a narrow escape. Father says there was never such imminent danger, and such miraculous escape. Father and Mr. Frink took charge of the fire—or rather of the *water,* since fire usually takes care of itself. The men all worked like heroes, and after the fire was out father gave commands to have them march to Howe's where an entertainment was provided for them. After the whole was over they gave "three cheers for Edward Dickinson," and three more for the insurance company. On the whole, it is very wonderful that we didn't all burn up, and we ought to hold our tongues and be very thankful. If there *must* be a fire, I'm sorry it couldn't wait until you had

245

got home, because you seem to enjoy such things so very much. . . .

To her brother Austin
[Written after a visit of the sisters in Boston, September, 1851.]

We have got home, dear Austin. It is very lonely here—I have tried to make up my mind which was better, home and parents and the country, or city and smoke and dust shared with the only being whom I can call my brother. The scales *don't* poise very evenly, but so far as I can judge, the balance is in your favor. . . .

Vinnie and I came safely, and met with no mishap—the bouquet was not withered nor was the bottle cracked. It was fortunate for the freight car that Vinnie and I were there, ours being the only baggage passing along the line. The folks looked very funny who travelled with us that day—they were dim and faded, like folks passed away—the conductor seemed so grand with about half a dozen tickets which he dispersed and demanded in a very small space of time—I judged that the minority were travelling that day, and couldn't hardly help smiling at our ticket friend, however sorry I was at the small amount of people passing along his way. He looked as if he wanted to make an apology for not having more travellers to keep him company.

The route and the cars seemed strangely—there were no boys with fruit, there were no boys with pamphlets; one fearful little fellow ventured into the car with what appeared to be publications and tracts; he offered them to no one, and no one inquired for them, and he seemed greatly relieved that no one wanted to buy them. . . . Mother sends much love, and Vinnie.

Your lonely sister
Emily

Oct. 2 [1851]

. . . You say we mustn't trouble to send you any fruit, also your clothes must give us no uneasiness. I don't ever want to have you say any more such things. They make me feel like crying. If you'd only teased us for it, and declared that you would have it, I shouldn't have cared so much that we could find no way to send you any, but you resign so cheerfully your birthright of purple grapes, and do not so much as murmur at the departing peaches, that I hardly can taste the one or drink the juice of the other. They are so beautiful, Austin, —we have such an abundance "while you perish with hunger." . . .

The peaches are very large—one side a rosy cheek, and the other a golden, and that peculiar coat of velvet and of down which makes a peach so beautiful. The grapes, too, are fine, juicy, and *such* a purple—I fancy the robes of kings are not a tint more royal. The vine looks like a kingdom, with ripe round grapes for kings, and hungry mouths for subjects—the first instance on record of subjects devouring kings! You *shall* have some grapes, dear Austin, if I have to come on foot in order to bring them to you.

The apples are very fine—it isn't quite time to pick them— the cider is almost done—we shall have some I guess by Saturday, at any rate Sunday noon. The vegetables are not gathered, but will be before very long. The horse is doing nicely; he travels "like a bird" to use a favorite phrase of your delighted mother's. You ask about the leaves—shall I say they are falling? They had begun to fall before Vinnie and I came home, and we walked up the steps through little brown ones rustling. . . .

Vinnie tells me she has detailed the news—she reserved the deaths for me, thinking I might fall short of my usual letter somewhere. In accordance with her wishes I acquaint you with the decease of your aged friend Deacon ———. He had no disease that we know of, but gradually went out. . . . Monday evening we were all startled by a violent church-bell ringing, and thinking of nothing but fire, rushed out in the street to see. The sky was a beautiful red, bordering on a crimson, and rays of a gold pink color were constantly shooting off from a kind of sun in the centre. People were alarmed at this beautiful phenomenon, supposing that fires somewhere were coloring the sky. The exhibition lasted for nearly fifteen minutes, and the streets were full of people wondering and admiring. Father happened to see it among the very first, and rang the bell himself to call attention to it. You will have a full account from the pen of Mr. Trumbull, who, I have not a doubt, was seen with a long lead pencil a-noting down the sky at the time of its highest glory. . . . You will be here now so soon—we are impatient for it—we want to see you, Austin, how much I cannot say here.

Your affectionate
Emily

To her brother Austin
[Amherst, October, 1851]

. . . The breakfast is so warm, and pussy is here a-singing, and the tea-kettle sings too, as if to see which was loudest, and I am so afraid lest kitty should be beaten—yet a shadow falls upon my morning picture—where is the youth so bold, the bravest of our fold—a seat is empty here—spectres sit in your chair, and now and then nudge father with their long, bony elbows. I wish you were here, dear Austin; the dust falls on the bureau in your deserted room, and gay, frivolous spiders spin away in the corners. I don't go there after dark whenever I can help it, for the twilight seems to pause there, and I am half afraid; and if ever I have to go, I hurry with all my might, and never look behind me, for I know who I should see.

Before next Tuesday—oh, before the coming stage, will I not brighten and brush it, and open the long-closed blinds, and with a sweeping broom will I not bring each spider down from its home so high, and tell it it may come back again when master has gone—and oh, I will bid it to be a tardy spider, to tarry on the way; and I will think my eye is fuller than sometimes, though *why* I cannot tell, when it shall rap on the window and come to live again. I am so happy when I know how soon you are coming that I put away my sewing and go out in the yard to think. I have tried to delay the frosts, I have coaxed the fading flowers, I thought I *could* detain a few of the crimson leaves until you had smiled upon them; but their companions call them, and they cannot stay away.

You will find the blue hills, Austin, with the autumnal shadows silently sleeping on them, and there will be a glory lingering round the day, so you'll know autumn has been here; and the setting sun will tell you, if you don't get home till evening. . . . I thank you for such a long letter, and yet if I might choose, the next should be a longer. I think a letter just about three days long would make me happier than any other kind of one, if you please,—dated at Boston, but thanks be to our Father you may conclude it here. Everything has changed since my other letter,—the doors are shut this morning, and all the kitchen wall is covered with chilly flies who are trying to warm themselves,—poor things, they do not understand that there are no summer mornings remaining to them and me, and they have a bewildered air which is really very droll, didn't one feel sorry for them. You would say 'twas a gloomy morning if you were sitting here, —the frost has been severe, and the few lingering leaves seem anxious to be going, and wrap their faded cloaks more closely about them as if to shield them from the chilly northeast wind. The earth looks like some poor old lady who by dint of pains has bloomed e'en till now, yet in a forgetful moment a few silver hairs from out her cap come stealing, and she tucks them back so hastily and thinks nobody sees. The cows are going to pasture, and little boys with their hands in their pockets are whistling to try to keep warm. Don't think that the sky will frown so the day when you come home! She will smile and look happy, and be full of sunshine then, and even should she frown upon her child returning, there is another sky, ever serene and fair, and there is another sunshine, though it be darkness there; never mind faded forests, Austin, never mind silent fields—*here* is a little forest, whose leaf is ever green; here is a brighter garden, where not a frost has been; in its unfading flowers I hear the bright bee hum; prithee, my brother, into *my* garden come!

Your very affectionate sister

To her brother Austin
[Amherst, November 17, 1851]

Dear Austin,—We have just got home from meeting—it is very windy and cold—the hills from our kitchen window are just crusted with snow, which with their blue mantillas makes them seem so beautiful. You sat just here last Sunday, where I am sitting now; and our voices were nimbler than our pens can be, if they try never so hardly. I should be quite sad to-day, thinking about last Sunday, didn't another Sabbath smile at me so pleasantly, promising me on its word to present you here again when "six days' work is done."

Father and mother sit in state in the sitting-room perusing such papers, only, as they are well assured, have nothing carnal in them; Vinnie is eating an apple which makes me think of gold, and accompanying it with her favorite *Observer,* which, if you recollect, deprives us many a time of her sisterly society. Pussy hasn't returned from the afternoon assembly, so you have us all just as we are at present. We were very glad indeed to hear from you so soon, glad that a cheerful fire met you at the door. I *do* well remember how chilly the west wind blew, and how everything shook and rattled before I went to sleep, and I often thought of you in the midnight car, and hoped you were not lonely. . . . We are thinking most of Thanksgiving than anything else just now—how full will be the circle, less then by none—how the things will smoke—how the board will groan with the thousand savory viands—how when the day is done, lo, the evening cometh, laden with merrie laugh and happy conversation, and then the sleep and the dream each of a knight or "Ladie"—how I love to see them, a beautiful company coming down the hill which men call the Future, with their hearts full of joy and their hands of gladness. Thanksgiving indeed to a family united once more together before they go away. . . . Don't mind the days—some of them are long ones, but who cares for length when breadth is in store for him? Or who minds the cross who knows he'll have a crown? I wish I could imbue you with all the strength and courage which can be given men—I wish I could assure you of the constant remembrance of those you leave at home—I wish—but oh! how vainly— that I could bring you back again and never more to stray. You are tired now, dear Austin, with my incessant din, but I can't help saying any of these things.

The very warmest love from Vinnie and every one of us. I am never ready to go.

Reluctant
Emily

To her brother Austin
[1851]

Did you think I was tardy, Austin? For two Sunday afternoons it has been so cold and cloudy that I didn't feel in my very happiest mood, and so I did not write until next Monday morning, determining in my heart never to write to you in any but cheerful spirits.

Even this morning, Austin, I am not in merry case, for it snows slowly and solemnly, and hardly an outdoor thing can be seen a-stirring—now and then a man goes by with a large cloak wrapped around him, and shivering at that; and now and then a stray kitten out on some urgent errand creeps through the flakes and crawls so fast as *may* crawl half frozen away. I am glad for the sake of your body that you are not here this morning, for it is a trying time for fingers and toes—for the heart's sake I would verily have you here. You know there are winter mornings when the cold without only adds to the warm within, and the more it snows and the harder it blows brighter the fires blaze, and chirps more merrily the "cricket on the hearth." It is hardly cheery enough for such a scene this morning, and yet methinks it would be if you were only here. The future full of sleigh-rides would chase the gloom from our minds which only deepens and darkens with every flake that falls.

Black Fanny would "toe the mark" if you should be here to-morrow; but as the prospects are, I presume Black Fanny's hoofs will not attempt to fly. Do you have any snow in Boston? Enough for a ride, I hope, for the sake of "Auld Lang Syne." Perhaps the "ladie" of curls would not object to a drive. . . . We miss you more and more, we do not become accustomed to separation from you. I almost wish sometimes we needn't miss you so much, since duty claims a year of you entirely to herself; and then again I think that it is pleasant to miss you if you must go away, and I would not have it otherwise, even if I could. In every pleasure and pain you come up to our minds so wishfully—we know you'd enjoy our joy, and if you were with us, Austin, we could bear little trials more cheerfully. . . . When I know of anything funny I am just as apt to cry, far more so than to laugh, for I know who loves jokes best, and who is not here to enjoy them. We don't have many jokes, though, now, it is pretty much all sobriety; and we do not have much poetry, father having made up his mind that it's pretty much all real life. Father's real life and mine sometimes come into collision but as yet escape unhurt. . . . I am so glad you are well and in such happy spirits—both happy and well is a great comfort to us when you are far away.

Emilie

. . . Since we have written you the grand railroad deci-
sion is made, and there is great rejoicing throughout this
town and the neighboring; that is, Sunderland, Montague,
and Belchertown. Everybody is wide awake, everything
is stirring, the streets are full of people walking cheer-
ingly, and you should really be here to partake of the jubilee.
The event was celebrated by D. Warner and cannon; and
the silent satisfaction in the hearts of all is its crowning
attestation.

Father is really sober from excessive satisfaction, and bears
his honors with a most becoming air. Nobody believes it yet,
it seems like a fairy tale, a most miraculous event in the lives
of us all. The men begin working next week; only think of it,
Austin; why, I verily believe we shall fall down and worship
the first "son of Erin" that comes, and the first sod he turns
will be preserved as an emblem of the struggle and victory of
our heroic fathers. Such old fellows as Col. S. and his wife
fold their arms complacently and say, "Well, I declare, we
have got it after all." Got it, *you* good-for-nothings! and so
we have, in spite of sneers and pities and insults from all
around; and we will keep it too, in spite of earth and heaven!
How I wish you were here—it is really too bad, Austin, at
such a time as now. I miss your big hurrahs, and the famous
stir you make upon all such occasions; but it is a comfort to
know that you are here—that your whole soul is here, and
though apparently absent, yet present in the highest and the
truest sense. . . .

Emilie

A valentine to Mr. William Howland, 1852.

Sic transit gloria mundi,
How doth the busy bee—
Dum vivimus vivamus,
I stay mine enemy.

Oh, *veni, vidi, vici,*
Oh, *caput, cap-a-pie,*
And oh, *memento mori*
When I am far from thee.

Hurrah for Peter Parley,
Hurrah for Daniel Boone,
Three cheers, sir, for the gentlemen
Who first observed the moon.

Peter put up the sunshine,
Pattie arrange the stars,
Tell Luna tea is waiting,
And call your brother Mars.

Put down the apple, Adam,
And come away with me;
So shall thou have a pippin
From off my father's tree.

I climb the hill of science,
I "view the landscape o'er,"
Such transcendental prospect
I ne'er beheld before.

Unto the Legislature
My country bids me go.
I'll take my india-rubbers,
In case the wind should blow.

During my education,
It was announced to me
That gravitation, stumbling,
Fell from an apple tree.

The earth upon its axis
Was once supposed to turn,
By way of a gymnastic
In honor to the sun.

It was the brave Columbus,
A-sailing on the tide,
Who notified the nations
Of where I would reside.

Mortality is fatal,
Gentility is fine,
Rascality heroic,
Insolvency sublime.

Our fathers being weary
Lay down on Bunker Hill,
And though full many a morning,
Yet they are sleeping still.

The trumpet, sir, shall wake them,
In dream I see them rise,
Each with a solemn musket
A-marching to the skies.

A coward will remain, sir,
Until the fight is done,
But an immortal hero
Will take his hat and run.

Good-by, sir, I am going—
My country calleth me.
Allow me, sir, at parting
To wipe my weeping e'e.

In token of our friendship
Accept this *Bonnie Doon,*
And when the hand that plucked it
Has passed beyond the moon,

The memory of my ashes
Will consolation be.
Then farewell, Tuscarora,
And farewell, sir, to thee.

To her brother Austin
[Amherst, March, 1852]

. . . It's a glorious afternoon—the sky is blue and warm—
the wind blows just enough to keep the clouds sailing, and
the sunshine—oh *such* sunshine! It isn't like gold, for gold is
dim beside it; it isn't like anything which you or I have seen!
It seems to me "Ik Marvel" was born on such a day; I only
wish you were here. Such days were made on purpose for
you and me; then what in the world are you gone for? Oh,
dear, I do not know, but this I do know, that if wishing
would bring you home, you were here to-day. Is it pleasant
in Boston? *Of course* it isn't, though. I might have known
more than to make such an inquiry. No doubt the streets are
muddy, and the sky some dingy hue, and I can think just how
everything bangs and rattles, and goes rumbling along
through stones and plank and clay! I don't feel as if I could
have you there, possibly, another day. I'm afraid you'll turn
into a bank, or a Pearl Street counting-room, if you have not
already assumed some monstrous shape, living in such a
place.

Let me see—April; three weeks until April—the very first
of April—well, perhaps that will do, only be sure of the
week, the *whole* week, and nothing but the week. If they
make new arrangements, give my respects to them, and tell
them old arrangements are good enough for you, and you

will have them; then if they raise the wind, why, let it blow—there's nothing more excellent than a breeze now and then!

What a time we shall have Fast day, after we get home from meeting—why, it makes me dance to think of it; and Austin, if I dance so many days beforehand, what will become of me when the hour really arrives? I don't know, I'm sure; and I don't care, much, for that or for anything else but get you home. . . . Much love from mother and Vinnie; we are now pretty well, and our hearts are set on April, the *very first* of April!

Emilie

To her brother Austin
[March 24, 1852]

You wouldn't think it was spring, Austin, if you were at home this morning, for we had a great snowstorm yesterday, and things are all white this morning. It sounds funny enough to hear birds singing and sleigh-bells at a time. But it won't last long, so you needn't think 'twill be winter at the time when you come home.

I waited a day or two, thinking I might hear from you, but you will be looking for me, and wondering where I am, so I sha'n't wait any longer. We're rejoiced that you're coming home—the first thing we said to father when he got out of the stage was to ask if you were coming. I was sure you would all the while, for father said "of course you would," he should "consent to no other arrangement," and as you say, Austin, "what father says he means." How very soon it will be now—why, when I really think of it, how near and how happy it is! My heart grows light so fast that I could mount a grasshopper and gallop around the world, and not fatigue him any! The sugar weather holds on, and I do believe it will stay until you come. . . . "Mrs. S." is very feeble; "can't bear allopathic treatment, can't have homoeopathic, don't want hydropathic," oh, what a pickle she is in! Shouldn't think she would deign to live, it is so decidedly

vulgar! They have not yet concluded where to move—Mrs.
W. will perhaps obtain board in the celestial city, but I'm
sure I can't imagine what will become of the rest. . . .
Much love from us all.

Emilie

To her brother Austin
[March 18, 1853]

Dear Austin,—I presume you remember a story that Vinnie
tells of a breach of promise case where the correspondence
between the parties consisted of a reply from the girl to one
she had never received but was daily expecting. Well, *I* am
writing an answer to the letter I haven't had, so you will see
the force of the accompanying anecdote. I have been looking
for you ever since despatching my last, but this is a fickle
world, and it's a great source of complacency that 'twill all
be burned up by and by. I should be pleased with a line when
you've published your work to father, if it's perfectly conve-
nient!

Your letters are very funny indeed—about the only jokes
we have, now you are gone, and I hope you will send us one
as often as you can. Father takes great delight in your re-
marks to him—puts on his spectacles and reads them o'er
and o'er as if it was a blessing to have an only son. He reads
all the letters you write, as soon as he gets them, at the post-
office, no matter to whom addressed; then he makes me read
them aloud at the supper table again, and when he gets home
in the evening, he cracks a few walnuts, puts his spectacles
on, and with your last in his hand, sits down to enjoy the
evening. . . . I believe at this moment, Austin, that there's
nobody living for whom father has such respect as for you.
But my paper is getting low, and I must hasten to tell you
that we are very happy to hear good news from you, that we
hope you'll have pleasant times and learn a great deal while
you're gone, and come back to us greater and happier for the
life lived at Cambridge. We miss you more and more. I wish

that we could see you, but letters come the next—write them often, and tell us everything.

Affectionately

Emilie

To Dr. and Mrs. J. G. Holland
[1853]

Dear Dr. and Mrs. Holland,—dear Minnie—it is cold to-night, but the thought of you so warm, that I sit by it as a fireside, and am never cold any more. I love to write to you — it gives my heart a holiday and sets the bells to ringing. If prayers had any answers to them, you were all here to-night, but I seek and I don't find, and knock and it is not opened. Wonder if God is just—presume He is, however, and 'twas only a blunder of Matthew's.

I think mine is the case, where when they ask an egg, they get a scorpion, for I keep wishing for you, keep shutting up my eyes and looking toward the sky, asking with all my might for you, and yet you do not come. I wrote to you last week, but thought you would laugh at me, and call me senti-mental, so I kept my lofty letter for "Adolphus Hawkins, Esq."

If it wasn't for broad daylight, and cooking-stoves, and roosters, I'm afraid you would have occasion to smile at my letters often, but so sure as "this mortal" essays immortality, a crow from a neighboring farm-yard dissipates the illusion, and I am here again.

And what I mean is this—that I thought of you all last week, until the world grew rounder than it sometimes is, and I broke several dishes.

Monday, I solemnly resolved I would be *sensible,* so I wore thick shoes, and thought of Dr. Humphrey, and the Moral Law. One glimpse of "The Republican" makes me break things again—I read in it every night.

Who writes those funny accidents, where railroads meet each other unexpectedly, and gentlemen in factories get their heads cut off quite informally? The author, too, relates them in such a sprightly way, that they are quite attractive. Vinnie was disappointed to-night, that there were not more accidents—I read the news aloud, while Vinnie was sewing. "The Republican" seems to us like a letter from you, and we break the seal and read it eagerly. . . .

Vinnie and I talked of you as we sewed, this afternoon. I said—"how far they seem from us," but Vinnie answered me "only a little way." . . . I'd love to be a bird or bee, that whether hum or sing, still might be near you.

Heaven is large—is it not? Life is short too, isn't it? Then when one is done, is there not another, and—and—then if God is willing, we are neighbors then. Vinnie and mother send their love. Mine too is here. My letter as a bee, goes laden. Please love us and remember us. Please write us very soon, and tell us how you are. . . .

Affectionately
Emilie

To her brother Austin
[April, 1853]

I rather thought from your letter to me that my essays, together with the lectures at Cambridge, were too much for you, so I thought I would let you have a little vacation; but you must have got rested now, so I shall renew the series. Father was very severe to me; he thought I'd been trifling with you, so he gave me quite a trimming about "Uncle Tom" and "Charles Dickens" and those "modern literati" who, he says, are nothing, compared to past generations who flourished when he was a boy. Then he said there were "somebody's rev-e-ries," he didn't know whose they were, that he thought were very ridiculous—so I'm quite in disgrace at present, but I think of that "pinnacle" on which you always mount when anybody insults you, and that's quite a comfort to me . . .

Emilie

To her brother Austin
[June, 1853, after a celebration of the opening of a
railroad to New London]

. . . The New London day passed off grandly, so all the
people said. It was pretty hot and dusty, but nobody cared
for that. Father was, as usual, chief marshal of the day, and
went marching around with New London at his heels like
some old Roman general upon a triumph day. Mrs. H. got a
capital dinner, and was very much praised. Carriages flew
like sparks, hither and thither and yon, and they all said
'twas fine. I "spose" it was. I sat in Professor Tyler's woods
and saw the train move off, and then came home again for
fear somebody would see me, or ask me how I did. Dr. Hol-
land was here, and called to see us—was very pleasant in-
deed, inquired for you, and asked mother if Vinnie and I
might come and see them in Springfield. . . . We all send
you our love.

Emilie

To her brother Austin
[Postmarked, July 2, 1853]

. . . Some of the letters you've sent us we have received,
and thank you for affectionately. Some we have not re-
ceived, but thank you for the memory, of which the emblem
perished. Where all those letters go, yours and ours, some-
body surely knows, but we do not. There's a new postmaster
to-day, but we don't know who's to blame. You never wrote
me a letter, Austin, which I liked half so well as the
one father brought me. We think of your coming home
with a great deal of happiness, and are glad you want to
come.

Father said he never saw you looking in better health or
seeming in finer spirits. He didn't say a word about the Hip-
podrome or the Museum, and he came home so stern that
none of us dared to ask him, and besides grandmother was

261

here, and you certainly don't think I'd allude to a Hippo-
drome in the presence of that lady! I'd as soon think of pop-
ping fire-crackers in the presence of Peter the Great. But
you'll tell us when you get home—how soon—how soon!
. . . I admire the "Poems" very much. We all send our love
to you—shall write you again Sunday.

Emilie

To her brother Austin
[January, 1854]

I have had some things from you to which I perceive no
meaning. They either were very vast, or they didn't mean
anything, I don't know certainly which. What did you
mean by a note you sent me day before yesterday? Father
asked me what you wrote, and I gave it to him to read.
He looked very much confused, and finally put on his spec-
tacles, which didn't seem to help him much—I don't think
a telescope would have assisted him. I hope you will write
to me—I love to hear from you, and now Vinnie is gone
I shall feel very lonely. . . . Love for them all if there
are those to love and think of me, and more and most for
you, from

Emily

To Dr. and Mrs. J. G. Holland
[1854]

Dear Friends,—I thought I would write again. I write you
many letters with pens which are not seen. Do you receive
them?

I think of you all to-day, and dreamed of you last night.

When father rapped on my door to wake me this morning,
I was walking with you in the most wonderful garden, and

helping you pick—roses, and though we gathered with all our might, the basket was never full. And so all day I pray that I may walk with you, and gather roses again, and as night draws on, it pleases me, and I count impatiently the hours 'tween me and the darkness, and the dream of you and the roses, and the basket never full.

God grant the basket fill not, till, with hands purer and whiter, we gather flowers of gold in baskets made of pearl; higher—higher! It seems long since we heard from you—long, since how little Annie was, or any one of you—so long since Cattle Show, when Dr. Holland was with us. Oh, it always seems a long while from our seeing you, and even when at your house, the nights seemed much more long than they're wont to do, because separated from you. I want so much to know if the friends are all well in that dear cot in Springfield—and if well whether happy, and happy—*how* happy, and why, and what bestows the joy? And then those other questions, asked again and again, whose answers are so sweet, do they love—remember us—wish sometimes we were there? Ah, friends—dear friends—perhaps my queries tire you, but I so long to know.

The minister to-day, not our own minister, preached about death and judgment, and what would become of those, meaning Austin and me, who behaved improperly—and somehow the sermon scared me, and father and Vinnie looked very solemn as if the whole was true, and I would not for worlds have them know that it troubled me, but I longed to come to you, and tell you all about it, and learn how to be better. He preached such an awful sermon though, that I didn't much think I should ever see you again until the Judgment Day, and then you would not speak to me, according to his story. The subject of perdition seemed to please him, somehow. It seems very solemn to me. I'll tell you all about it, when I see you again.

I wonder what you are doing to-day—if you have been to meeting? To-day has been a fair day, very still and blue. To-night the crimson children are playing in the West, and to-morrow will be colder. How sweet if I could see you, and talk of all these things! Please write us very soon. The days with you last September seem a great way off, and to meet you again delightful. I am sure it won't be long before we sit together.

Then will I not repine, knowing that bird of mine, though flown—learneth beyond the sea, melody new for me, and will return.

Affectionately
Emily

To Mrs. J. G. Holland
[March, 1855]

Philadelphia

Dear Mrs. Holland and Minnie, and Dr. Holland too—I have stolen away from company to write a note to you; and to say that I love you still.

I am not at home—I have been away just five weeks to-day, and shall not go quite yet back to Massachusetts. Vinnie is with me here, and we have wandered together into many new ways.

We were three weeks in Washington, while father was there, and have been two in Philadelphia. We have had many pleasant times, and seen much that is fair, and heard much that is wonderful—many sweet ladies and noble gentlemen have taken us by the hand and smiled upon us pleasantly— and the sun shines brighter for our way thus far.

I will not tell you what I saw—the elegance, the grandeur; you will not care to know the value of the diamonds my Lord and Lady wore, but if you haven't been to the sweet Mount Vernon, then I *will* tell you how on one soft spring day we glided down the Potomac in a painted boat, and jumped upon the shore—how hand in hand we stole along up a tangled pathway till we reached the tomb of General George Washington, how we paused beside it, and no one spoke a word, then hand in hand, walked on again, not less wise or sad for that marble story; how we went within the door—

raised the latch he lifted when he last went home—thank the Ones in Light that he's since passed in through a brighter wicket! Oh, I could spend a long day, if it did not weary you, telling of Mount Vernon—and I will sometime if we live and meet again, and God grant we shall!

I wonder if you have all forgotten us, we have stayed away so long. I hope you haven't I tried to write so hard before I went from home, but the moments were so busy, and then they *flew* so. I was sure when days *did* come in which I was less busy, I should seek your forgiveness, and it did not occur to me that you might not forgive me. Am I too late to-day? Even if you are angry, I shall keep praying you, till from very weariness, you will take me in. It seems to me many a day since we were in Springfield, and Minnie and the *dumb-bells* seem as vague—as vague; and sometimes I wonder if I ever dreamed—then if I'm dreaming now, then if I *always* dreamed, and there is not a world, and not these darling friends, for whom I would not count my life too great a sacrifice. Thank God there is a world, and that the friends we love dwell forever and ever in a house above. I fear I grow incongruous, but to meet my friends does delight me so that I quite forget time and sense and so forth.

Now, my precious friends, if you won't forget me until I get home, and become more sensible, I will write again, and more properly. Why didn't I ask before, if you were well and happy?

Forgetful
Emilie

To Mrs. J. G. Holland
[Written in 1856, soon after the family moved back into the house built by E.D.'s grandfather]

Your voice is sweet, dear Mrs. Holland. I wish I heard it oftener. One of the mortal musics Jupiter denies, and when indeed its gentle measures fall upon my ear, I stop the birds to listen. Perhaps you think I have no bird—and this is rhetoric—pray, Mr. Whately, what is that upon the cherry tree? Church is done, and the winds blow, and Vinnie is in that pallid land the simple call "sleep." They will be wiser by and by. We shall all be wiser! While I sit in the snows, the summer day on which you came and the bees and the south wind, seem fabulous as heaven seems to a sinful world—and I keep remembering it till it assumes a spectral air, and nods and winks at me, and then all of you turn to phantoms and vanish slow away . . .

I cannot tell you how we moved. I had rather not remember. I believe my "effects" were brought in a bandbox, and the "deathless me," on foot, not many moments after. I took at the time a memorandum of my several senses, and also of my hat and coat, and my best shoes—but it was lost in the *mêlée,* and I am out with lanterns, looking for myself.

Such wits as I reserved, are so badly shattered that repair is useless—and still I can't help laughing at my own catastrophe. I supposed we were going to make a "transit," as heavenly bodies did—but we came budget by budget, as our fellows do, till we fulfilled the pantomime contained in the word "moved." It is a kind of *gone-to-Kansas* feeling, and if I sat in a long wagon, with my family tied behind, I should suppose without doubt that I was a party of emigrants!

They say that "home is where the heart is." I think it is where the *house* is, and the adjacent buildings.

But, my dear Mrs. Holland, I have another story, and lay my laughter all away, so that I can sigh. Mother has been an invalid since we came *home,* and Vinnie and I "regulated," and Vinnie and I "got settled," and still we keep our father's house, and mother lies upon the lounge, or sits in her easy-chair. I don't know what her sickness is, for I am but a simple child, and frightened at myself. I often wish I was a grass, or a toddling daisy, whom all these problems of the dust might not terrify—and should my own machinery get slightly out of gear *please,* kind ladies and gentlemen, some one stop the wheel,—for I know that with belts and bands of gold, I shall whizz triumphant on the new stream! Love for you—love for Dr. Holland—thanks for his exquisite hymn—tears for your sister in sable, and kisses for Minnie and the bairns.

From your mad Emilie

To Mrs. J. G. Holland
[Late summer, 1856]

Don't tell, dear Mrs. Holland, but wicked as I am, I read my Bible sometimes, and in it as I read to-day, I found a verse like this, where friends should "go no more out"; and there were "no tears," and I wished as I sat down to-night that we were *there*—not *here*—and that wonderful world had commenced, which makes such promises, and rather than to write you, I were by your side, and the "hundred and forty and four thousand" were chatting pleasantly, yet not disturbing us. And I'm half tempted to take my seat in that Paradise of which the good man writes, and begin forever and ever *now*, so wondrous does it seem. My only sketch, profile, of Heaven is a large, blue sky, bluer and larger than the *biggest* I have seen in June, and in it are my friends—all of them—every one of them—those who are with me now, and those who were "parted" as we walked, and "snatched up to Heaven."

If roses had not faded, and frosts had never come, and one had not fallen here and there whom I could not waken, there were no need of other Heaven than the one below—and if God had been here this summer, and seen the things that *I* have seen—I guess that He would think His Paradise superfluous. Don't tell Him, for the world, though, for after all He's said about it, I should like to see what He *was* building for us, with no hammer, and no stone, and no journeyman either. Dear Mrs. Holland, I love, to-night—love you and Dr. Holland, and "time and sense"—and fading things, and things that do *not* fade.

I'm so glad you are not a blossom, for those in my garden fade, and then a "reaper whose name is Death" has come to get a few to help him make a bouquet for himself, so I'm glad you are not a rose—and I'm glad you are not a bee, for where they go when summer's done, only the thyme knows, and even were you a robin, when the west winds came, you would coolly wink at me, and away, some morning!

As "little Mrs. Holland," then, I think I love you most, and trust that tiny lady will dwell below while we dwell, and when with many a wonder we seek the new Land, *her* wistful face, *with* ours, shall look the last upon the hills, and first upon—well, *Home!*

Pardon my sanity, Mrs. Holland, in a world *in*sane, and love me if you will, for I had rather *be* loved than to be called a king in earth, or a lord in Heaven.

Thank you for your sweet note—the clergy are very well. Will bring such fragments from them as shall seem to me good. I kiss my paper here for you and Dr. Holland—would it were cheeks instead.

Dearly
Emilie

P.S. The bobolinks have gone.

To Dr. and Mrs. J. G. Holland
[1858]

Dear Hollands,—Good-night! I can't stay any longer in a world of death. Austin is ill of fever. I buried my garden last week—our man, Dick, lost a little girl through the scarlet fever. I thought perhaps that *you* were dead, and not knowing the sexton's address, interrogate the daisies. Ah! dainty—dainty Death! Ah! democratic Death! Grasping the proudest zinnia from my purple garden,—then deep to his bosom calling the serf's child!

Say, is he everywhere? Where shall I hide my things? Who is alive? The woods are dead. Is Mrs. H. alive? Annie and Katie—are they below, or received to nowhere?

I shall not tell how short time is, for I was told by lips

which sealed as soon as it was said, and the open revere the shut. You were not here in summer. *Summer?* My memory flutters—had I—was there a summer? You should have seen the fields go—gay little entomology! Swift little ornithology! Dancer, and floor, and cadence quite gathered away, and I, a phantom, to you a phantom, rehearse the story! An orator of feather unto an audience of fuzz,—and pantomimic plaudits. "Quite as good as a play," indeed! Tell Mrs. Holland she is mine.

Ask her if *vice versa?* Mine is but just the thief's request— "Remember me to-day." Such are the bright chirographies of the "Lamb's Book." Good-night! My ships are in!—My window overlooks the wharf! One yacht, and a man-of-war; two brigs and a schooner! "Down with the topmast! Lay her a' hold, a' hold!"

Emilie

To Mrs. Samuel Bowles
[1858]

Dear Mrs. Bowles,—Since I have no sweet flower to send you, I enclose my heart. A little one, sunburnt, half broken sometimes, yet close as the spaniel to its friends. Your flowers come from heaven, to which, if I should ever go, I will pluck you palms.

My words are far away when I attempt to thank you, so take the silver tear instead, from my full eye.

You have often remembered me.

I have little dominion. Are there not wiser than I, who, with curious treasure, could requite your gift?

Angels fill the hand that loaded

Emily's

To Samuel Bowles
[1858]

Dear Mr. Bowles,—I got the little pamphlet. I think you sent it to me, though unfamiliar with your hand—I may mistake. Thank you, if I am right. Thank you, if not, since here I find bright pretext to ask you how you are to-night, and for the health of four more, elder and minor Mary, Sallie and Sam, tenderly to inquire.

I hope your cups are full.

I hope your vintage is untouched. In such a porcelain life one likes to be *sure* that all is well lest one stumble upon one's hopes in a pile of broken crockery.

My friends are my estate. Forgive me then the avarice to hoard them! They tell me those were poor early have different views of gold. I don't know how that is.

God is not so wary as we, else He would give us no friends, lest we forget Him! The charms of the heaven in the bush are superseded, I fear, by the heaven in the hand, occasionally.

Summer stopped since you were here. Nobody noticed her —that is, no men and women. Doubtless, the fields are rent by petite anguish, and "mourners go about" the woods. But this is not for us. Business enough indeed, our stately resurrection! A special courtesy, I judge, from what the clergy say! To the "natural man" bumblebees would seem an improvement, and a spicing of birds, but far be it from me to impugn such majestic tastes!

Our pastor says we are a "worm." How is that reconciled? "Vain, sinful worm" is possibly of another species.

Do you think we shall "see God"? Think of Abraham strolling with Him in genial promenade!

The men are mowing the second hay. The cocks are smaller than the first, and spicier. I would distil a cup, and bear to all my friends, drinking to her no more astir, by beck, or burn, or moor!

Good-night, Mr. Bowles. This is what they say who come back in the morning; also the closing paragraph on repealed lips. Confidence in daybreak modifies dusk.

Blessings for Mrs. Bowles, and kisses for the bairns' lips. We want to see you, Mr. Bowles, but spare you the rehearsal of "familiar truths."

Good-night
Emily

To Mrs. Samuel Bowles
[1859]

Dear Mrs. Bowles, You send sweet messages. Remembrance is more sweet than robins in May orchards.

I love to trust that round bright fires, some, braver than I, take my pilgrim name. How are papa, mamma, and the little people? . . .

It storms in Amherst five days—it snows, and then it rains, and then soft fogs like veils hang on all the houses, and then the days turn topaz, like a lady's pin.

Thank you for bright bouquet, and afterwards verbena. I made a plant of a little bough of yellow heliotrope which the bouquet bore me, and call it Mary Bowles. It is many days since the summer day when you came with Mr. Bowles, and before another summer day it will be many days. My garden is a little knoll with faces under it, and only the pines sing tunes, now the birds are absent. I cannot walk to the distant friends on nights piercing as these, so I put both hands on the window-pane, and try to think how birds fly, and imitate, and fail, like Mr. "Rasselas." I could make a balloon of a dandelion, but the fields are gone, and only "Professor Lowe" remains to weep with me. If I built my house I should like to call you. I talk of all these things with Carlo, and his eyes grow meaning, and his shaggy feet keep a slower pace. Are you safe to-night? I hope you may be glad. I ask God on my knee to send you much prosperity, few winter days, and long suns. I have a childish hope to gather all I love together and sit down beside and smile. . . .

Will you come to Amherst? The streets are very cold now,

but we will make you warm. But if you never came, perhaps you could write a letter, saying how much you would like to, if it were "God's will." I give good-night, and daily love to you and Mr. Bowles.

Emilie

To Samuel Bowles
[1859]

Friend, Sir,—I did not see you. I am very sorry. Shall I keep the wine till you come again, or send it in by Dick? It is now behind the door in the library, also an unclaimed flower. I did not know you were going so soon. Oh! my tardy feet.

Will you not come again?

Friends are gems, infrequent. Potosi is a care, sir. I guard it reverently, for I could not afford to be poor now, after affluence. I hope the hearts in Springfield are not so heavy as they were. God bless the hearts in Springfield.

I am happy you have a horse. I hope you will get stalwart, and come and see us many years.

I have but two acquaintances, the "quick and the dead" and would like more.

I write you frequently, and am much ashamed. My voice is not quite loud enough to cross so many fields, which will, if you please, apologize for my pencil.

Will you take my love to Mrs. Bowles, whom I remember every day?

Emilie

Vinnie hallos from the world of night-caps, "don't forget her love."

To Kate Scott Turner (Anthon)
[1859]

Katie,—Last year at this time I did not miss you, but positions shifted, until I hold your black in strong hallowed remembrance, and trust my colors are to you tints slightly beloved.

You cease, indeed, to talk, which is a custom prevalent among things parted and torn, but shall I class this, dear, among elect exceptions, and bear you just as usual unto the kind Lord?

We dignify our faith when we can cross the ocean with it, though most prefer ships.

How do you do this year? . . . How many years, I wonder, will sow the moss upon them, before we bind again, a little altered, it may be, elder a little it *will* be, and yet the same, as suns which shine between our lives and loss, and violets—not last year's, but having the mother's eyes.

Do you find plenty of food at home? Famine is unpleasant.

It is too late for frogs—or what pleases me better, dear, not quite early enough! The pools were full of you for a brief period, but that brief period blew away, leaving me with many stems, and but a few foliage! Gentlemen here have a way of plucking the tops of the trees, and putting the fields in their cellars annually, which in point of taste is execrable, and would they please omit, I should have fine vegetation and foliage all the year round, and never a winter month. Insanity to the sane seems so unnecessary—but I am only one, and they are "four and forty," which little affair of numbers leaves me impotent. Aside from this, dear Katie, inducements to visit Amherst are as they were—I am pleasantly located in the deep sea, but love will row you out, if her hands are strong, and don't wait till I land, for I'm going ashore on the other side.

                                                              Emilie

To Mrs. Samuel Bowles
[1859]

I should like to thank dear Mrs. Bowles for the little book, except my cheek is red with shame because I write so often. Even the "lilies of the field" have their dignities.

Why did you bind it in green and gold? The *immortal* colors. I take it for an emblem. I never read before what Mr. Parker wrote.

I heard that he was "poison." Then I like poison very well. Austin stayed from service yesterday afternoon, and I . . . found him reading my Christmas gift. . . . I wish the "faith of the fathers" didn't wear brogans, and carry blue umbrellas. I give you all "New Year!" I think you kept gay Christmas, from the friend's account, and can only sigh with one not present at "John Gilpin," "and when he next doth ride a race," etc. You picked your berries from my holly. Grasping Mrs. Bowles!

To-day is very cold, yet have I much bouquet upon the window-pane of moss and fern. I call them saints' flowers, because they do not romp as other flowers do, but stand so still and white.

The snow is very tall, . . . which makes the trees so low that they tumble my hair, when I cross the bridge.

I think there will be no spring this year, the flowers are gone so far. Let us have spring in our heart, and never mind the orchises! . . . Please have my love, mother's, and Vinnie's. Carlo sends a brown kiss, and pussy a gray and white one, to each of the children.

Please, now I write so often, make lamplighter of me, then I shall not have lived in vain.

Dear Mrs. Bowles, dear Mr. Bowles, dear Sally—Sam and Mamie, now all shut your eyes, while I do benediction!

Lovingly

Emily

To Kate Scott Turner (Anthon)
[1859]

. . . Sweet at my door this March night another candidate.
Go home! We don't like Katies here! Stay! My heart votes for
you, and what am I, indeed, to dispute her ballot!

What are your qualifications? Dare you dwell in the East
where we dwell? Are you afraid of the sun? When you hear
the new violet sucking her way among the sods, shall you be
resolute? All we are strangers, dear, the world is not ac-
quainted with us, because we are not acquainted with her;
and pilgrims. Do you hesitate? And soldiers, oft—some of us
victors, but those I do not see to-night, owing to the smoke.
We are hungry, and thirsty, sometimes, we are barefoot and
cold—will you still come?

Then, bright I record you—Kate, gathered in March! It is a
small bouquet, dear, but what it lacks in size it gains in fade-
lessness. Many can boast a hollyhock, but few can bear a
rose! And should new flower smile at limited associates, pray
her remember were there many, they were not worn upon the
breast, but tilled in the pasture. So I rise wearing her—so I
sleep holding,—sleep at last with her fast in my hand, and
wake bearing my flower.

Emilie

To Louise Norcross
[January, 1859]

Since it snows this morning, dear Loo, too fast for interrup-
tion, put your brown curls in a basket, and come and sit with
me.

I am sewing for Vinnie, and Vinnie is flying through the
flakes to buy herself a little hood. It's quite a fairy morning,
and I often lay down my needle, and "build a castle in the
air" which seriously impedes the sewing project. What if I
pause a little longer, and write a note to you! Who will be the
wiser? I have known little of you, since the October morning

when our families went out driving, and you and I in the dining-room decided to be distinguished. It's a great thing to be "great," Loo, and you and I might tug for a life, and never accomplish it, but no one can stop our looking on, and you know some cannot sing, but the orchard is full of birds, and we all can listen. What if we learn, ourselves, some day! Who indeed knows?—said you had many little cares; I hope they do not fatigue you. I would not like to think of Loo as weary, now and then. Sometimes *I* get tired, and I would rather none I love would understand the word. . . .

Do you still attend Fanny Kemble? "Aaron Burr" and father think her an "animal," but I fear zoölogy has few such instances. I have heard many notedly *bad* readers, and a fine one would be almost a fairy surprise. When will you come again, Loo? For you remember, dear, you are one of the ones from whom I do not run away! I keep an ottoman in my heart exclusively for you. My love for your father and Fannie.

Emily

To *Louise Norcross*
[Early summer, 1859]

Dear Loo,—You did not acknowledge my vegetable; perhaps you are not familiar with it. I was reared in the garden, you know. It was to be eaten with mustard! Bush eighty feet high, just under chamber window—much used at this season when other vegetables are gone. You should snuff the hay if you were here to-day, infantile as yet, homely, as cubs are prone to be, but giving brawny promise of hay-cocks by and by. "Methinks I see you," as school-girls say, perched upon a cock with the "latest work," and confused visions of bumblebees tugging at your hat. Not so far off, cousin, as it used to be, that vision and the hat. It makes me feel so hurried, I run and brush my hair so to be all ready.

I enjoy much with a precious fly, during sister's absence, not one of your blue monsters, but a timid creature, that hops from pane to pane of her white house, so very cheer-fully, and hums and thrums, a sort of speck piano. Tell Vinnie I'll kill him the day she comes, for I sha'n't need him any more, and she don't mind flies!

Tell Fannie and papa to come with the sweet-williams.

Tell Vinnie I counted three peony noses, red as Sammie Matthews's, just out of the ground, and get her to make the accompanying face. "By-Bye."

Emily

To Dr. and Mrs. J. G. Holland
[Autumn, 1859]

Dear Hollands,—Belong to me! We have no fires yet, and the evenings grow cold. To-morrow, stoves are set. How many barefoot shiver I trust their Father knows who saw not fit to give them shoes.

Vinnie is sick to-night, which gives the world a russet tinge, usually so red. It is only a headache, but when the head aches next to you, it becomes important. When she is well, time leaps. When she is ill, he lags, or stops entirely.

Sisters are brittle things. God was penurious with me, which makes me shrewd with Him.

One is a dainty sum! One bird, one cage, one flight; one song in those far woods, as yet suspected by faith only!

This is September, and you were coming in September. Come! Our parting is too long. There has been frost enough. We must have summer now, and "whole legions" of daisies.

The gentian is a greedy flower, and overtakes us all. Indeed, this world is short, and I wish, until I tremble, to touch the ones I love before the hills are red—are gray—are white —are "born again"! If we knew how deep the crocus lay, we never should let her go. Still, crocuses stud many mounds whose gardeners till in anguish some tiny, vanished bulb.

We saw you that Saturday afternoon, but heedlessly forgot to ask where you were going, so did not know, and could not write. Vinnie saw Minnie flying by, one afternoon at Palmer.

She supposed you were all there on your way from the sea, and untied her fancy! To say that her fancy wheedled her is superfluous.

We talk of you together, then diverge on life, then hide in you again, as a safe fold. Don't leave us long, dear friends! You know we're children still, and children fear the dark.

Are you well at home? Do you work now? Has it altered much since I was there? Are the children women, and the women thinking it will soon be afternoon? We will help each other bear our unique burdens.

Is Minnie with you now? Take her our love, if she is. Do her eyes grieve her now? Tell her she may have half ours.

Mother's favorite sister is sick, and mother will have to bid her good-night. It brings mists to us all;—the aunt whom Vinnie visits, with whom she spent, I fear, her last inland Christmas. Does God take care of those at sea? My aunt is such a timid woman!

Will you write to us? I bring you all their loves—*many*. They tire me.

Emilie

To Kate Scott Turner (Anthon)
[1860]

The prettiest of pleas, dear, but with a lynx like me quite unavailable. Finding is slow, facilities for losing so frequent, in a world like this, I hold with extreme caution. A prudence so astute may seem unnecessary, but plenty moves those most, dear, who have been in want, and Saviour tells us, Kate, the poor are always with us. Were you ever poor? I have been a beggar, and rich to-night, as by God's leave I believe I am, the "lazzaroni's" faces haunt, pursue me still!

You do not yet "dislimn," Kate. Distinctly sweet your face stands in its phantom niche—I touch your hand—my cheek your cheek—I stroke your vanished hair. Why did you enter, sister, since you must depart? Had not its heart been torn enough but you must send your shred?

Oh, our condor Kate! Come from your crags again! Oh, dew upon the bloom fall yet again a summer's night! Of such have been the frauds which have vanquished faces, sown plant of flesh the churchyard plats, and occasioned angels.

There is a subject, dear, on which we never touch. Ignorance of its pageantries does not deter me. I too went out to meet the dust early in the morning. I too in daisy mounds possess hid treasure, therefore I guard you more. You did not tell me you had once been a "millionaire." Did my sister think that opulence could be mistaken? Some trinket will remain, some babbling plate or jewel.

I write you from the summer. The murmuring leaves fill up the chinks through which the winter red shone when Kate was here, and F—— was here, and frogs sincerer than our own splash in their Maker's pools. It's but a little past, dear, and yet how far from here it seems, fled with the snow! So through the snow go many loving feet parted by "Alps." How brief, from vineyards and the sun!

Parents and Vinnie request love to be given girl.

Emilie

To Louise Norcross
[1860]

The little "apple of my eye" is not dearer than Loo; she knows I remember her,—why waste an instant in defence of an absurdity? My birds fly far off, nobody knows where they go to, but you see I know they are coming back, and other people don't, that makes the difference.

I've had a curious winter, very swift, sometimes sober, for I haven't felt well, much, and March amazes me! I didn't think of it, that's all! Your "hay" don't look so dim as it did at one time. I hayed a little for the horse two Sundays ago, and mother thought it was summer, and set one plant outdoors which she brought from the deluge, but it snowed since, and we have fine sleighing, now, on *one* side of the road, and wheeling on the other, a kind of variegated turn-pike quite picturesque to see!

You are to have Vinnie, it seems, and I to tear my hair, or engage in any other vocation that seems fitted to me. Well, the earth is round, so if Vinnie rolls your side sometimes, 'tisn't strange; I wish I were there too, but the geraniums felt so I couldn't think of leaving them, and one minute carnation pink cried, till I shut her up—see box!

Now, my love, robins, for both of you, and when you and Vinnie sing at sunrise on the apple boughs, just cast your eye to my twig.

Poor Plover

To Samuel Bowles
[1860]

Dear Mr. Bowles,—Thank you.

> Faith is a fine invention
> When gentlemen can see!
> But microscopes are prudent
> In an emergency!

You spoke of the "East." I have thought about it this winter.

Don't you think you and I should be shrewder to take the mountain road?

That bareheaded life, under the grass, worries one like a wasp.

The rose is for Mary.

Emily

To Mrs. Samuel Bowles
[August, 1861]

Mary,—I do not know of you, a long while. I remember you—several times. I wish I knew if you kept me? The doubt, like the mosquito, buzzes round my faith. We are all human, Mary, until we are divine, and to some of us, that is far off, and to some as near as the lady ringing at the door; perhaps *that's* what alarms. I say I will go myself—I cross the river, and climb the fence—now I am at the gate, Mary —now I am in the hall—now I am looking your heart in the eye!

Did it wait for me—did it go with the company? Cruel company, who have the stocks, and farms, and creeds—and *it* has just its heart! I hope you are glad, Mary; no pebble in the brook to-day—no film on noon.

I can think how you look; you can't think how I look; I've got more freckles, since you saw me, playing with the school-boys; then I pare the "Juneating" to make the pie, and get my fingers "tanned."

Summer went very fast—she got as far as the woman from the hill, who brings the blueberry, and that is a long way. I shall have no winter this year, on account of the soldiers. Since I cannot weave blankets or boots, I thought it best to omit the season. Shall present a "memorial" to God when the maples turn. Can I rely on your "name"?

How is your garden, Mary? Are the pinks true, and the sweet williams faithful? I've got a geranium like a sultana, and when the humming-birds come down, geranium and I shut our eyes, and go far away.

Ask "Mamie" if I shall catch her a butterfly with a vest like a Turk? I will, if she will build him a house in her "morning-glory."

Vinnie would send her love, but she put on a white frock, and went to meet to-morrow—a few minutes ago; mother would send her love, but she is in the "eave spout," sweeping up a leaf that blew in last November; I brought my own, myself, to you and Mr. Bowles.

Please remember me, because I remember you—always. . . .

Don't cry, dear Mary. Let us do that for you, because you are too tired now. We don't know how dark it is, but if you are at sea, perhaps when we say that we are there, you won't be as afraid.

The waves are very big, but every one that covers you, covers us, too.

Dear Mary, you can't see us, but we are close at your side. May we comfort you?

Lovingly
Emily

To Louise and Fannie Norcross
[1861]

. . . —fed greedily upon "Harper's Magazine's" while here. Suppose he is restricted to Martin Luther's works at home. It is a criminal thing to be a boy in a godly village, but maybe he will be forgiven.

. . . The seeing pain one can't relieve makes a demon of one. If angels have the heart beneath their silver jackets, I think such things could make them weep, but Heaven is so cold! It will never look kind to me that God, who causes all, denies such little wishes. It could not hurt His glory, unless it were a lonesome kind. I 'most conclude it is.

. . . Thank you for the daisy. With nature in my ruche I shall not miss the spring. What would become of us, dear, but for love to reprieve our blunders?

. . . I'm afraid that home is 'most done, but do not say I fear so. Perhaps God will be better. They're happy, you know. That makes it doubtful. Heaven hunts round for those that find itself below, and then it snatches.

. . . Think Emily lost her wits—but she found 'em, likely. Don't part with wits long in this neighborhood.

. . . Your letters are all real, just the tangled road children walked before you, some of them to the end, and others but a little way, even as far as the fork in the road. That Mrs.

Browning fainted, we need not read "Aurora Leigh" to know, when she lived with her English aunt; and George Sand "must make no noise in her grandmother's bedroom." Poor children! Women, now, queens, now! And one in the Eden of God. I guess they both forget that now, so who knows but we, little stars from the same night, stop twinkling at last? Take heart, little sister, twilight is but the short bridge, and the moon stands at the end. If we can only get to her! Yet, if she sees us fainting, she will put out her yellow hands. . . .

To Louise Norcross
[December, 1861]

Dear Peacock,—I received your feather with profound emotion. It has already surmounted a work, and crossed the Delaware. Doubtless you are moulting *à la* canary bird—hope you will not suffer from the reduction of plumage these December days. The latitude is quite stiff for a few nights, and gentlemen and ladies who go barefoot in our large cities must find the climate uncomfortable. A land of frosts and zeros is not precisely the land for me; hope you find it congenial. I believe it is several hundred years since I met you and Fannie, yet I am pleased to say, you do not become dim; I think you rather brighten as the hours fly. I should love to see you dearly, girls; perhaps I may, before south winds, but I feel rather confused to-day, and the future looks "higglety-pigglety."

You seem to take a smiling view of my finery. If you knew how solemn it was to me, you might be induced to curtail your jests. My sphere is doubtless calicoes, nevertheless I thought it meet to sport a little wool. The mirth it has occasioned will deter me from further exhibitions! Won't you tell "the public" that at present I wear a brown dress with a cape if possible browner, and carry a parasol of the same! We have at present one cat, and twenty-four hens, who do nothing so vulgar as lay an egg, which checks the ice-cream tendency.

I miss the grasshoppers much, but suppose it is all for the best. I should become too much attached to a trotting world.

My garden is all covered up by snow; picked gilliflower Tuesday, now gilliflowers are asleep. The hills take off their purple frocks, and dress in long white nightgowns.

There is something fine and something sad in the year's toilet. . . .

We often talk of you and your father these new winter days. Write, dear, when you feel like it.

Lovingly
Emily

To Louise Norcross
[December 29, 1861]

. . . Your letter didn't surprise me, Loo; I brushed away the sleet from eyes familiar with it—looked again to be sure I read it right—and then took up my work hemming strings for mother's gown. I think I hemmed them faster for knowing you weren't coming, my fingers had nothing else to do. . . . Odd, that I, who say "no" so much, cannot bear it from others. Odd, that I, who run from so many, cannot brook that one turn from me. Come when you will, Loo, the hearts are never shut here. I don't remember "May." Is that the one that stands next April? And is that the month for the river-pink?

Mrs. Adams had news of the death of her boy to-day, from a wound at Annapolis. Telegram signed by Frazer Stearns. You remember him. Another one died in October—from fever caught in the camp. Mrs. Adams herself has not risen from bed since then. "Happy new year" step softly over such doors as these! "Dead! Both her boys! One of them shot by the sea in the East, and one of them shot in the West by the sea." . . . Christ be merciful! Frazer Stearns is just leaving

Annapolis. His father has gone to see him to-day. I hope that ruddy face won't be brought home frozen. Poor little widow's boy, riding to-night in the mad wind, back to the village burying-ground where he never dreamed of sleeping! Ah! the dreamless sleep! . . .

Emilie

To an unknown recipient
[1861]

. . . If you saw a bullet hit a bird, and he told you he wasn't shot, you might weep at his courtesy, but you would certainly doubt his word. Thomas's faith in anatomy was stronger than his faith in faith. . . . Vesuvius don't talk— Ætna don't. One of them said a syllable, a thousand years ago, and Pompeii heard it and hid forever. She couldn't look the world in the face afterward, I suppose. Bashful Pompeii! . . .

To Samuel Bowles
[1861]

Dear Friend,—You remember the little "meeting" we held for you last spring? We met again, Saturday.

'Twas May when we "adjourned," but then adjourns are all. The meetings were alike, Mr. Bowles.

The topic did not tire us, so we chose no new. We voted to remember you so long as both should live, including immortality; to count you as ourselves, except sometimes more tenderly, as now, when you are ill, and we, the haler of the two —and so I bring the bond we sign so many times, for you to read when chaos comes, or treason, or decay, still witnessing for morning. . . . We hope our joy to see you gave of its own degree to you. We pray for your new health, the prayer that goes not down when they shut the church. We offer

you our cups—stintless, as to the bee,—the lily, her new liquors.
Would you like summer? Taste of ours.
Spices? Buy here!
Ill! We have berries, for the parching!
Weary! Furloughs of down!
Perplexed! Estates of violet trouble ne'er looked on!
Captive! We bring reprieve of roses!
Fainting! Flasks of air!
Even for Death, a fairy medicine.
But, which is it, sir?

Emily

To Dr. and Mrs. J. G. Holland
[1862]

Dear Friends,—I write to you. I receive no letter.

I say "they dignify my trust." I do not disbelieve. I go again. *Cardinals* wouldn't do it. Cockneys wouldn't do it, but I can't *stop* to strut, in a world where bells toll. I hear through visitor in town, that "Mrs. Holland is not strong." The little peacock in me, tells me not to inquire again. Then I remember my tiny friend—how brief she is—how dear she is, and the peacock quite dies away. Now, you need not speak, for perhaps you are weary, and "Herod" requires all your thought, but if you are *well*—let Annie draw me a little picture of an erect flower; if you are *ill,* she can hang the flower a little on one side!

Then, I shall understand, and you need not stop to write me a letter. Perhaps you laugh at me! Perhaps the whole United States are laughing at me too! *I* can't stop for that! *My* business is to love. I found a bird, this morning, down—down—on a little bush at the foot of the garden, and wherefore sing, I said, since nobody *hears?*

One sob in the throat, one flutter of bosom—*"My* business is to *sing"*—and away she rose! How do I know but cheru-

bim, once, themselves, as patient, listened, and applauded
her unnoticed hymn?

Emily

To Samuel Bowles
[Spring, 1862]

Dear Friend,—The hearts in Amherst ache to-night—you
could not know how hard. They thought they could not
wait, last night, until the engine sang a pleasant tune that
time, because that you were coming. The flowers waited, in
the vase, and love got peevish, watching. A railroad person
rang, to bring an evening paper—Vinnie tipped pussy over,
in haste to let you in, and I, for joy and dignity, held tight in
my chair. My hope put out a petal.

You would come, to-day,—but . . . we don't believe it,
now; "Mr. Bowles not coming!" Wouldn't you, to-morrow,
and this but be a bad dream, gone by next morning?

Please do not take our *spring* away, since you blot summer
out! We cannot count our tears for this, because they drop so
fast. . . .

Dear friend, we meant to make you brave, but moaned
before we thought. . . . If you'll be sure and get well, we'll
try to bear it. If we could only care the less, it would be so
much easier. Your letter troubled my throat. It gave that little
scalding we could not know the reason for till we grew far
up.

I must do my good-night in crayon I meant to in red.

Love for Mary.

Emily

To Mrs. Samuel Bowles
[Written after Mr. Bowles had sailed for Europe, early summer, 1862]

Dear Mary,—When the best is gone, I know that other things are not of consequence. The heart wants what it wants, or else it does not care.

You wonder why I write so. Because I cannot help. I like to have you know some care—so when your life gets faint for its other life, you can lean on us. We won't break, Mary. We look very small, but the reed can carry weight.

Not to see what we love is very terrible, and talking doesn't ease it, and nothing does but just itself. The eyes and hair we chose are all there are—to us. Isn't it so, Mary?

I often wonder how the love of Christ is done when that below holds so.

I hope the little "Robert" coos away the pain. Perhaps your flowers help, some. . . .

The frogs sing sweet to-day—they have such pretty, lazy times—how nice to be a frog! . . .

Mother sends her love to you—she has a sprained foot, and can go but little in the house, and not abroad at all.

Don't dishearten, Mary, we'll keep thinking of you. Kisses for all.

Emily

To Samuel Bowles
[August, 1862]

—Vinnie is trading with a tin peddler—buying water-pots for me to sprinkle geraniums with when you get home next winter, and she has gone to the war.

Summer isn't so long as it was, when we stood looking at it before you went away; and when I finish August, we'll hop the autumn very soon, and then 'twill be yourself.

I don't know how many will be glad to see you,—because I

never saw your whole friends, but I have heard that in large cities noted persons chose you—though how glad those I know will be, is easier told.

I tell you, Mr. Bowles, it is a suffering to have a sea—no care how blue—between your soul and you.

The hills you used to love when you were in Northampton, miss their old lover, could they speak; and the puzzled look deepens in Carlo's forehead as the days go by and you never come.

I've learned to read the steamer place in newspapers now. It's 'most like shaking hands with you, or more like your ringing at the door.

We reckon your coming by the fruit. When the grape gets by, and the pippin and the chestnut—when the days are a little short by the clock, and a little long by the want—when the sky has new red gowns and a purple bonnet—then we say you will come. I am glad that kind of time goes by.

It is easier to look behind at a pain, than to see it coming.

A soldier called, a morning ago, and asked for a nosegay to take to battle. I suppose he thought we kept an aquarium.

How sweet it must be to one to come home, whose home is in so many houses, and every heart a "best room." I mean you, Mr. Bowles. . . . Have not the clovers names to the bees?

Emily

To Louise and Fannie Norcross
[May, 1863]

. . . The nights turned hot, when Vinnie had gone, and I must keep no window raised for fear of prowling "booger," and I must shut my door for fear front door slide open on me at the "dead of night," and I must keep "gas" burning to light the danger up, so I could distinguish it—these gave me a snarl in the brain which don't unravel yet, and that old nail in my breast pricked me; these, dear, were my cause. Truth is so best of all I wanted you to know. Vinnie will tell of her visit. . . .

About Commencement, children, I can have no doubt, if you should fail me then, my little life would fail of itself. Could you only lie in your little bed and smile at me, that would be support. Tell the doctor I am inexorable, besides I shall heal you quicker than he. You need the balsam word. And who is to cut the cake, ask Fannie, and chirp to those trustees? Tell me, dears, by the coming mail, that you will not fail me. . . .

Jennie Hitchcock's mother was buried yesterday, so there is one orphan more, and her father is very sick besides. My father and mother went to the service, and mother said while the minister prayed, a hen with her chickens came up, and tried to fly into the window. I suppose the dead lady used to feed them, and they wanted to bid her good-by.

> Life is death we're lengthy at,
> Death the hinge to life.

Love from all
Emily

To Louise and Fannie Norcross
[Autumn, 1863]

. . . I should be wild with joy to see my little lovers. The writing them is not so sweet as their two faces that seem so small way off, and yet have been two weeks from me—two wishful, wandering weeks. Now, I begin to doubt if they ever came.

I bid the stiff "good-night" and the square "good-morning" to the lingering guest, I finish mamma's sack, all but the overcasting—that fatal sack, you recollect. I pick up tufts of mignonette, and sweet alyssum for winter, dim as winter seems these red, and gold, and ribbon days.

I am sure I feel as Noah did, docile, but somewhat sceptic, under the satinet.

No frost at our house yet. Thermometer frost, I mean. . . .

L—— goes to Sunderland, Wednesday, for a minute or two; leaves here at half-past six—what a fitting hour—and will breakfast the night before; such a smart atmosphere! The trees stand right up straight when they hear her boots, and will bear crockery wares instead of fruit, I fear. She hasn't starched the geraniums yet, but will have ample time, unless she leaves before April. Emily is very mean, and her children in dark mustn't remember what she says about damsel.

Grateful for little notes, and shall ask for longer when my birds locate. Would it were here. Three sisters are prettier than one. . . . Tabby is a continual shrine, and her jaunty ribbons put me in mind of fingers far out at sea. Fannie's admonition made me laugh and cry too. In the hugest haste, and the engine waiting.

Emily

To Thomas Wentworth Higginson
[1863]

Dear Friend—You were so generous to me, that if possible I offended you, I could not too deeply apologize.

To doubt my high behavior is a new pain. I could be honorable no more, till I asked you about it. I know not what to deem myself—yesterday "your scholar," but might I be the one you to-night forgave, 'tis a better honor. Mine is but just the thief's request.

Please, sir, hear

"Barabbas"

The possibility to pass
Without a moment's hell
Into conjecture's presence,
Is like a face of steel

That suddenly looks into ours
With a metallic grin;
The cordiality of Death
Who drills his welcome in.

To Louise and Fannie Norcross
[1863]

. . . Would it interest the children to know that crocuses
come up, in the garden off the dining-room, and a fuchsia,
that pussy partook, mistaking it for strawberries? And that
we have primroses, like the little pattern sent in last winter's
note, and heliotrope by the aprons full—the mountain
colored one—and a jasmine bud, you know the little odor
like Lubin—and gilliflowers, magenta, and few mignonette,
and sweet alyssum bountiful, and carnation buds?

Will it please them to know that the ice-house is filled, to
make their tumblers cool next summer, and once in a while a
cream? . . .

Love, dears, from us all, and won't you tell us how you
are? We seem to hear so little.

Emily

To Louise and Fannie Norcross
[1864]

. . . Sorrow seems more general than it did, and not the
estate of a few persons, since the war began; and if the an-
guish of others helped one with one's own, now would be
many medicines.

'Tis dangerous to value, for only the precious can alarm. I
noticed that Robert Browning had made another poem, and
was astonished—till I remembered that I, myself, in my
smaller way, sang off charnel steps. Every day life feels

mightier, and what we have the power to be, more stupendous.

To her sister Lavinia
[1864]

. . . Father told me you were going. I wept for the little
plants, but rejoiced for you. Had I loved them as well as I
did, I could have begged you to stay with them, but they are
foreigners now, and all, a foreigner. I have been sick so long
I do not know the sun. I hope they may be alive, for home
would be strange except them, now the world is dead.

Anna Norcross lives here since Saturday, and two new
people more, a person and his wife, so I do little but fly, yet
always find a nest. I shall go home in two weeks. You will get
me at Palmer? . . .

Sister

To Mrs. J. G. Holland
[1865]

Dear Sister,—Father called to say that our steelyard was
fraudulent, exceeding by an ounce the rates of honest men.
He had been selling oats. I cannot stop smiling, though it is
hours since, that even our steelyard will not tell the truth.

Beside wiping the dishes for Margaret, I wash them now,
while she becomes Mrs. Lawler, vicarious papa to four previous
babes. Must she not be an adequate bride?

. . . I winced at her loss, because I was in the habit of her,
and even a new rolling-pin has an embarrassing element, but
to all except anguish, the mind soon adjusts.

It is also November. The noons are more laconic and the
sundowns sterner, and Gibraltar lights make the village foreign.
November always seemed to me the Norway of the
year. —is still with the sister who put her child in an ice nest
last Monday forenoon. The redoubtable God! I notice where

293

Death has been introduced, he frequently calls, making it desirable to forestall his advances.

It is hard to be told by the papers that a friend is failing, not even know where the water lies. Incidentally, only, that he comes to land. Is there no voice for these? Where is Love to-day?

Tell the dear Doctor we mention him with a foreign accent, party already to transactions spacious and untold. Nor have we omitted to breathe shorter for our little sister. Sharper than dying is the death for the dying's sake.

News of these would comfort, when convenient or possible.

Emily

To Louise Norcross
[January, 1865]

. . . I am glad my little girl is at peace. Peace is a deep place. Some, too faint to push, are assisted by angels.

I have more to say to you all than March has to the maples, but then I cannot write in bed. I read a few words since I came home—John Talbot's parting with his son, and Margaret's with Suffolk. I read them in the garret, and the rafters wept.

Remember me to your company, their Bedouin guest.

Every day in the desert, Ishmael counts his tents. New heart makes new health, dear.

Happiness is haleness. I dreamed last night I heard bees fight for pond-lily stamens, and waked with a fly in my room.

Shall you be strong enough to lift me by the first of April? I won't be half as heavy as I was before. I will be good and chase my spools.

I shall think of my little Eve going away from Eden. Bring me a jacinth for every finger, and an onyx shoe.

Emily

To Louise Norcross
[February, 1865]

All that my eyes will let me shall be said for Loo, dear little solid gold girl. I am glad to the foot of my heart that you will go to M——. It will make you warm. Touches "from home," tell Gungl, are better than "sounds."

You persuade me to speak of my eyes, which I shunned doing, because I wanted you to rest. I could not bear a single sigh should tarnish your vacation, but, lest through me one bird delay a change of latitude, I will tell you, dear.

The eyes are as with you, sometimes easy, sometimes sad. I think they are not worse, nor do I think them better than when I came home.

The snow-light offends them, and the house is bright; notwithstanding, they hope some. For the first few weeks I did nothing but comfort my plants, till now their small green cheeks are covered with smiles. . . . Go, little girl, to M——. Life is so fast it will run away, notwithstanding our sweetest *whoa.*

Already they love you. Be but the maid you are to me, and they will love you more.

Carry your heart and your curls, and nothing more but your fingers. Mr. D—— will ask for these every candlelight. How I miss ten robins that never flew from the rosewood nest!

To Mrs. J. G. Holland
[1866]

. . . February passed like a skate and I know March. Here is the "light" the stranger said "was not on sea or land." Myself could arrest it, but will not chagrin him.

. . . Cousin Peter told me the Doctor would address Commencement—trusting it insure you both for papa's *fête* I endowed Peter. We do not always know the source of the smile that flows to us . . .

My flowers are near and foreign, and I have but to cross the floor to stand in the Spice Isles.

The wind blows gay to-day and the jays bark like blue terriers.

I tell you what I see—the landscape of the spirit requires a lung, but no tongue. I hold you few I love, till my heart is red as February and purple as March.

Hand for the Doctor.

Emily

To Mrs. J. G. Holland
[1866]

Dear Sister,—After you went, a low wind warbled through the house like a spacious bird, making it high but lonely. When you had gone the love came. I supposed it would. The supper of the heart is when the guest has gone.

Shame is so intrinsic in a strong affection we must all experience Adam's reticence. I suppose the street that the lover travels is thenceforth divine, incapable of turnpike aims.

That you be with me annuls fear and I await Commencement with merry resignation. Smaller than David you clothe me with extreme Goliath.

Friday I tasted life. It was a vast morsel. A circus passed the house—still I feel the red in my mind though the drums are out.

The book you mention, I have not met. Thank you for tenderness.

The lawn is full of south and the odors tangle, and I hear to-day for the first the river in the tree.

You mentioned spring's delaying—I blamed her for the opposite. I would eat evanescence slowly.

Vinnie is deeply afflicted in the death of her dappled cat, though I convince her it is immortal which assists her some. Mother resumes lettuce, involving my transgression—suggestive of yourself, however, which endears disgrace.

"House" is being "cleaned." I prefer pestilence. That is more classic and less fell.

Yours was my first arbutus. It was a rosy boast.

I will send you the first witch hazel.

A woman died last week, young and in hope but a little while—at the end of our garden. I thought since of the power of Death, not upon affection, but its mortal signal. It is to us the Nile.

You refer to the unpermitted delight to be with those we love. I suppose that to be the license not granted of God.

Count not that far that can be had,
Though sunset lie between—
Nor that adjacent, that beside,
Is further than the sun.

Love for your embodiment of it.

Emily

To Mrs. J. G. Holland
[Replying to a letter addressed to both sisters, 1866]

Sister,—A mutual plum is not a plum. I was too respectful to take the pulp and do not like a stone.

Send no union letters. The soul must go by Death alone, so, it must by life, if it is a soul.

If a committee—no matter.

I saw the sunrise on the Alps since I saw you. Travel why to Nature, when she dwells with us? Those who lift their hats shall see her, as devout do God.

I trust you are merry and sound. The chances are all against the dear, when we are not with them, though paws of principalities cannot affront if we are by.

Dr. Vaill called here Monday on his way to your house to get the Doctor to preach for him. Shall search "The Republican" for a brief of the sermon. To-day is very homely and awkward as the homely are who have not mental beauty.

To Louise and Fannie Norcross
[Spring, 1870]

Dear Children,—I think the bluebirds do their work exactly like me. They dart around just so, with little dodging feet, and look so agitated. I really feel for them, they seem to be so tried.

The mud is very deep—up to the wagons' stomachs—arbutus making pink clothes, and everything alive.

Even the hens are touched with the things of Bourbon, and make republicans like me feel strangely out of scene.

Mother went rambling, and came in with a burdock on her shawl, so we know that the snow has perished from the earth. Noah would have liked mother.

I am glad you are with Eliza. It is next to shade to know that those we love are cool on a parched day. . . .

Father steps like Cromwell when he gets the kindlings.

Mrs. S—— gets bigger, and rolls down the lane to church like a reverend marble. Did you know that little Mrs. Holland was in Berlin for her eyes?

Did you know about Mrs. J——? She fledged her antique wings. 'Tis said that "nothing in her life became her like the leaving it" . . .

Emily

To Louise Norcross
[1870]

. . . I cooked the peaches as you told me, and they swelled to beautiful fleshy halves and tasted quite magic. The beans we fricasseed and they made a savory cream in cooking that "Aunt Emily" liked to sip. She was always fonder of julep food than of more substantial. Your remembrance of her is very sweetly touching.

Maggie is ironing, and a cotton and linen and ruffle heat makes the pussy's cheeks red. It is lonely without the birds

to-day, for it rains badly, and the little poets have no umbrel-
las. . . .
. . . Fly from Emily's window for Loo. Botanical name
unknown. [Enclosing a pressed insect.]

To Perez Cowan
[In reply to an announcement of his marriage, 1870]

Dear Peter,—It is indeed sweet news. I am proud of your
happiness. To Peter, and Peter's, let me give both hands. De-
light has no competitor, so it is always most.
    "Maggie" is a warm name. I shall like to take it.
    Home is the definition of God.

Emily

To Louise and Fannie Norcross
[1870]

Untiring Little Sisters,—What will I ever do for you, yet have
done the most, for love is that one perfect labor nought can
supersede. I suppose the pain is still there, for pain that is
worthy does not go so soon. The small can crush the great,
however, only temporarily. In a few days we examine, mus-
ter our forces, and cast it away. Put it out of your hearts,
children. Faith is too fair to taint it so. There are those in the
morgue that bewitch us with sweetness, but that which is
dead must go with the ground. There is a verse in the Bible
that says there are those who shall not see death. I suppose
them to be the faithful. Love will not expire. There was never
the instant when it was lifeless in the world, though the
quicker deceit dies, the better for the truth, who is indeed our
dear friend.
    I am sure you will gain, even from this wormwood. The
martyrs may not choose their food.

God made no act without a cause,
    Nor heart without an aim,
Our inference is premature,
    Our premises to blame.

. . . Sweetest of Christmas to you both, and a better year.

To Louise and Frances Norcross
[1870]

Dear Children,—When I think of your little faces I feel as the band does before it makes its first shout. . . .

Mother drives with Tim to carry pears to settlers. Sugar pears with hips like hams, and the flesh of bonbons. Vinnie fastens flowers from the frosts. . . .

Lifetime is for two, never for committee.

I saw your Mrs. H——. She looks a little tart, but Vinnie says makes excellent pies after one gets acquainted.

                                                        Emily

To Louise Norcross
[Spring, 1871]

The will is always near, dear, though the feet vary. The terror of the winter has made a little creature of me, who thought myself so bold.

Father was very sick. I presumed he would die, and the sight of his lonesome face all day was harder than personal trouble. He is growing better, though physically reluctantly. I hope I am mistaken, but I think his physical life don't want to live any longer. You know he never played, and the straightest engine has its leaning hour. Vinnie was not here. Now we will turn the corner. All this while I was with you all, much of every hour, wishing we were near enough to assist each other. Would you have felt more at home, to know we were both in extremity? That would be my only regret that I had not told you.

As regards the "pine" and the "jay," it is a long tryst, but I think they are able. I have spoken with them.

Of the "thorn," dear, give it to me, for I am strongest. Never carry what I can carry, for though I think I bend, something straightens me. Go to the "wine-press," dear, and come back and say has the number altered. I descry but one. What I would I cannot say in so small a place.

Interview is acres, while the broadest letter feels a bandaged place. . . .

Tell Fannie we hold her tight. Tell Loo love is oldest and takes care of us, though just now in a piercing place.

Emily

To Louise Norcross
[1872]

. . . An ill heart, like a body, has its more comfortable days, and then its days of pain, its long relapse, when rallying requires more effort than to dissolve life, and death looks choiceless.

Of Miss P—— I know but this, dear. She wrote me in October, requesting me to aid the world by my chirrup more. Perhaps she stated it as my duty, I don't distinctly remember, and always burn such letters, so I cannot obtain it now. I replied declining. She did not write to me again—she might have been offended, or perhaps is extricating humanity from some hopeless ditch. . . .

To Louise Norcross
[1872]

. . . How short it takes to go, dear, but afterward to come so many weary years—and yet 'tis done as cool as a general trifle. Affection is like bread, unnoticed till we starve, and then we dream of it, and sing of it, and paint it, when every urchin in the street has more than he can eat. We turn not older with years, but newer every day.

Of all these things we tried to talk, but the time refused us. Longing, it may be, is the gift no other gift supplies. Do you remember what you said the night you came to me? I secure that sentence. If I should see your face no more it will be your portrait, and if I should, more vivid than your mortal face. We must be careful what we say. No bird resumes its egg.

A word left careless on a page
May consecrate an eye,
When folded in perpetual seam
The wrinkled author lie.

Emily

To Fannie Norcross
[1873]

Thank you, dear, for the love. I am progressing timidly. Experiment has a stimulus which withers its fear.

This is the place they hoped before,
Where I am hoping now.
The seed of disappointment grew
Within a capsule gay,
Too distant to arrest the feet
That walk this plank of balm—
Before them lies escapeless sea—
The way is closed they came.

Since you so gently ask, I have had but one serious adventure—getting a nail in my foot, but Maggie pulled it out. It only kept me awake one night, and the birds insisted on sitting up, so it became an occasion instead of a misfortune.

There was a circus, too, and I watched it away at half-past three that morning. They said "hoy, hoy" to their horses.

Glad you heard Rubinstein. Grieved Loo could not hear him. He makes me think of polar nights Captain Hall could tell. Going from ice to ice! What an exchange of awe! . . .

Xerxes must go now and see to her worlds. You shall "taste," dear.

Lovingly

To Perez Cowan
[1873]

It is long since I knew of you, Peter, and much may have happened to both; but that is the rarest book, which, opened at whatever page, equally enchants us.

I hope that you have power, and as much of peace as in our deep existence may be possible.

To multiply the harbors does not reduce the sea.

We learn, through Cousin Montague, that you have lost your sister through that sweeter loss which we call gain.

I am glad she is glad.

Her early pain had seemed to me peculiarly cruel.

Tell her how tenderly we are pleased.

Recall me too to your other sisters, who though they may have mislaid me, I can always find; and include me to your sweet wife. We are daily reminded of you by the clergyman, Mr. Jenkins, whom you strongly resemble.

Thank you for the paper. It is homelike to know where you are.

We can almost hear you announce the text, when the air is clear; and how social if you should preach us a note some Sunday in recess!

Emily

To Louise and Fannie Norcross
[1873]

Spring is a happiness so beautiful, so unique, so unexpected, that I don't know what to do with my heart. I dare not take it, I dare not leave it—what do you advise?

Life is a spell so exquisite that everything conspires to break it.

"What do I think of 'Middlemarch'?" What do I think of glory—except that in a few instances this "mortal has already put on immortality."

George Eliot is one. The mysteries of human nature surpass the "mysteries of redemption," for the infinite we only suppose, while we see the finite. . . . I launch Vinnie on Wednesday; it will require the combined efforts of Maggie, Providence and myself, for whatever advances Vinnie makes in nature and art, she has not reduced departure to a science. . . .

Your loving
Emily

To Louise and Fannie Norcross
[1873]

Sisters,—I hear robins a great way off, and wagons a great way off, and rivers a great way off, and all appear to be hurrying somewhere undisclosed to me. Remoteness is the founder of sweetness; could we see all we hope, or hear the whole we fear told tranquil, like another tale, there would be madness near. Each of us gives or takes heaven in corporeal person, for each of us has the skill of life. I am pleased by your sweet acquaintance. It is not recorded of any rose that it failed of its bee, though obtained in specific instances through scarlet experience. The career of flowers differs from ours only in inaudibleness. I feel more reverence as I grow for these mute creatures whose suspense or transport may surpass my own . . .

Emily

To Louise and Fannie Norcross
[June, 1874]

You might not remember me, dears. I cannot recall myself. I
thought I was strongly built, but this stronger has under-
mined me.

We were eating our supper the fifteenth of June, and Aus-
tin came in. He had a despatch in his hand, and I saw by his
face we were all lost, though I didn't know how. He said that
father was very sick, and he and Vinnie must go. The train
had already gone. While horses were dressing, news came he
was dead.

Father does not live with us now—he lives in a new house.
Though it was built in an hour it is better than this. He
hasn't any garden because he moved after gardens were
made, so we take him the best flowers, and if we only knew
he knew, perhaps we could stop crying. . . . The grass be-
gins after Pat has stopped it.

I cannot write any more, dears. Though it is many nights,
my mind never comes home. Thank you each for the love,
though I could not notice it. Almost the last tune that he
heard was, "Rest from thy loved employ."

Emily

To Samuel Bowles
[1874]

I should think you would have few letters, for your own
are so noble that they make men afraid. And sweet as
your approbation is, it is had in fear, lest your depth convict
us.

You compel us each to remember that when water ceases
to rise, it has commenced falling. That is the law of flood.

The last day that I saw you was the newest and oldest of
my life.

Resurrection can come but once, first, to the same house.
Thank you for leading us by it.

Come always, dear friend, but refrain from going. You spoke of not liking to be forgotten. Could you, though you would?

Treason never knew you.

Emily

To Samuel Bowles
[1875]

Dear Friend,—It was so delicious to see you—a peach before the time—it makes all seasons possible, and zones a caprice.

We, who arraign the "Arabian Nights" for their understatement, escape the stale sagacity of supposing them sham.

We miss your vivid face, and the besetting accents you bring from your Numidian haunts.

Your coming welds anew that strange trinket of life which each of us wear and none of us own; and the phosphorescence of yours startles us for its permanence.

Please rest the life so many own—for gems abscond.

In your own beautiful words—for the voice is the palace of all of us,—

"Near, but remote."

Emily

To Louise and Fannie Norcross
[August, 1876]

Dear Cousins,—Mr. S—— had spoken with pleasure of you, before you spoke of him. Good times are always mutual; that is what makes good times. I am glad it cheered you.

We have had no rain for six weeks except one thunder shower, and that so terrible that we locked the doors, and the clock stopped—which made it like Judgment day. The heat is very great, and the grass so still that the flies speck it. I fear Loo will despair. The notices of the "fall trade" in the hurrying dailies, have a whiff of coolness.

Vinnie has a new pussy the color of Branwell Brontë's hair. She thinks it a little "lower than the angels," and I concur with her. You remember my ideal cat has always a huge rat in its mouth, just going out of sight—though going out of sight in itself has a peculiar charm. It is true that the unknown is the largest need of the intellect, though for it, no one thinks to thank God. . . . Mother is worn with the heat, but otherwise not altering. I dream about father every night, always a different dream, and forget what I am doing daytimes, wondering where he is. Without anybody, I keep thinking. What kind can that be?

Dr. Stearns died homelike, asked Eliza for a saucer of strawberries, which she brought him, but he had no hands. "In such an hour as ye think not" means something when you try it.

Lovingly
Emily

To Louise and Fannie Norcross
[November, 1876]

. . . Oh that beloved witch-hazel which would not reach me till part of the stems were a gentle brown, though one loved stalk as hearty as if just placed in the mail by the woods. It looked like tinsel fringe combined with staider fringes, witch and witching too, to my joyful mind.

I never had seen it but once before, and it haunted me like childhood's Indian pipe, or ecstatic puff-balls, or that mysterious apple that sometimes comes on river-pinks; and is there not a dim suggestion of a dandelion, if her hair were ravelled and she grew on a twig instead of a tube,—though this is timidly submitted. For taking Nature's hand to lead her to me, I am softly grateful—was she willing to come?

Though her reluctances are sweeter than other ones' avowals.

Trusty as the stars
Who quit their shining working
Prompt as when I lit them
In Genesis' new house,
Durable as dawn
Whose antiquated blossom
Makes a world's suspense
Perish and rejoice.

Love for the cousin sisters, and the lovely alien. . . .

Lovingly

Emily

To Thomas Wentworth Higginson
[1877]

Dear Friend,—Thank you for permission to write Mrs. Higginson. I hope I have not fatigued her—also for thinking of my brother, who is slowly better, and rides for an hour, kind days.

I am glad if I did as you would like. The degradation to displease you, I hope I may never incur.

Often, when troubled by entreaty, that paragraph of yours has saved me—"Such being the majesty of the art you presume to practise, you can at least take time before dishonoring it," and Enobarbus said, "Leave that which leaves itself."

I shall look with joy for the "little book" because it is yours, though I seek you in vain in the magazines where you once wrote. I recently found two papers of yours that were unknown to me, and wondered anew at your withdrawing thought so sought by others.

When flowers annually died and I was a child, I used to read Dr. Hitchcock's book on the "Flowers of North

America." This comforted their absence, assuring me they lived.

Your Scholar

To Thomas Wentworth Higginson
[Summer, 1878]

Dear Friend,—When you wrote you would come in November, it would please me it were November then—but the time has moved. You went with the coming of the birds—they will go with your coming, but to see you is so much sweeter than birds, I could excuse the spring.

With the bloom of the flower your friend loved, I have wished for her, but God cannot discontinue Himself.

Mr. Bowles was not willing to die.

When you have lost a friend, Master, you remember you could not begin again, because there was no world. I have thought of you often since the darkness, though we cannot assist another's night.

I have hoped you were saved.

That those have immortality with whom we talked about it, makes it no more mighty but perhaps more sudden. . . .

How brittle are the piers
On which our faith doth tread—
No bridge below doth totter so,
Yet none hath such a crowd.

It is as old as God—
Indeed, 'twas built by Him—
He sent His son to test the plank,
And he pronounced it firm.

I hope you have been well. I hope your rambles have been sweet, and your reveries spacious.

To have seen Stratford on Avon, and the Dresden Madonna, must be almost peace.

And perhaps you have spoken with George Eliot. Will you

"tell me about it"? Will you come in November, and will November come, or is this the hope that opens and shuts, like the eye of the wax doll?

Your Scholar

To Mrs. Edward Tuckerman
[August, 1878]

To see is perhaps never quite the sorcery that it is to surmise, though the obligation to enchantment is always binding.

It is sweet to recall that we need not retrench, as magic is our most frugal meal.

I fear you have much happiness, because you spend so much.

Would adding to it take it away, or is that a penurious question?

To cherish you is intuitive.

As we take Nature, without permission, let us covet you.

To Mrs. Samuel Bowles
[After the death of Mr. Bowles, January, 1878]

I hasten to you, Mary, because no moment must be lost when a heart is breaking, for though it broke so long, each time is newer than the last, if it broke truly. To be willing that I should speak to you was so generous, dear.

Sorrow almost resents love, it is so inflamed.

I am glad if the broken words helped you. I had not hoped so much, I felt so faint in uttering them, thinking of your great pain. Love makes us "heavenly" without our trying in the least. 'Tis easier than a Saviour—it does not stay on high and call us to its distance; its low "Come unto me" begins in every place. It makes but one mistake, it tells us it is "rest"— perhaps its toil is rest, but what we have not known we shall know again, that divine "again" for which we are all breathless.

I am glad you "work." Work is a bleak redeemer, but it does redeem; it tires the flesh so that can't tease the spirit.

Dear "Mr. Sam" is very near, these midwinter days. When purples come on Pelham, in the afternoon, we say "Mr. Bowles's colors." I spoke to him once of his Gem chapter, and the beautiful eyes rose till they were out of reach of mine, in some hallowed fathom.

Not that he goes—we love him more who led us while he stayed. Beyond earth's trafficking frontier, for what he moved, he made.

Mother is timid and feeble, but we keep her with us. She thanks you for remembering her, and never forgets you. . . . Your sweet "and left me all alone," consecrates your lips.

Emily

To Thomas Wentworth Higginson
[In acknowledgment of his *Short Studies of American Authors,* 1879]

Dear Friend,—Brabantio's gift was not more fair than yours, though I trust without his pathetic inscription, "Which but thou hast already, with all my heart I would keep from thee."

Of Poe, I know too little to think—Hawthorne appalls—entices.

Mrs. Jackson soars to your estimate lawfully as a bird, but of Howells and James one hesitates. Your relentless music dooms as it redeems.

Remorse for the brevity of a book is a rare emotion, though fair as Lowell's "sweet despair" in the "slipper hymn."

One thing of it we borrow
And promise to return,
The booty and the sorrow
Its sweetness to have known.

One thing of it we covet—
The power to forget,
The anguish of the avarice
Defrays the dross of it.

Had I tried before reading your gift to thank you, it had perhaps been possible, but I waited, and now it disables my lips.

Magic, as it electrifies, also makes decrepit. Thank you for thinking of me.

Your Scholar

To Louise and Fannie Norcross
[About July 4, 1879]

Dear Cousins,—Did you know there had been a fire here, and that but for a whim of the wind Austin and Vinnie and Emily would have all been homeless? But perhaps you saw "The Republican."

We were waked by the ticking of the bells,—the bells tick in Amherst for a fire, to tell the firemen.

I sprang to the window, and each side of the curtain saw that awful sun. The moon was shining high at the time, and the birds singing like trumpets.

Vinnie came soft as a moccasin, "Don't be afraid, Emily, it is only the fourth of July."

I did not tell that I saw it, for I thought if she felt it best to deceive, it must be that it was.

She took hold of my hand and led me into mother's room. Mother had not waked, and Maggie was sitting by her. Vinnie left us a moment, and I whispered to Maggie, and asked her what it was.

"Only Stebbins's barn, Emily"; but I knew that the right and left of the village was on the arm of Stebbins's barn. I could hear buildings falling, and oil exploding, and people walking and talking gayly, and cannon soft as velvet from parishes that did not know that we were burning up.

And so much lighter than day was it, that I saw a caterpillar measure a leaf far down in the orchard; and Vinnie kept saying bravely, "It's only the fourth of July."

It seemed like a theatre, or a night in London, or perhaps like chaos. The innocent dew falling "as if it thought no evil," . . . and sweet frogs prattling in the pools as if there were no earth.

At seven people came to tell us that the fire was stopped, stopped by throwing sound houses in as one fills a well.

Mother never waked, and we were all grateful; we knew she would never buy needle and thread at Mr. Cutler's store, and if it were Pompeii nobody could tell her.

The post-office is in the old meeting-house where Loo and I went early to avoid the crowd, and—fell asleep with the bumble-bees and the Lord God of Elijah.

Vinnie's "only the fourth of July" I shall always remember. I think she will tell us so when we die, to keep us from being afraid.

Footlights cannot improve the grave, only immortality.

Forgive me the personality; but I knew, I thought, our peril was yours.

Love for you each.

Emily

To Mrs. Samuel Bowles
[April, 1880]

Dear Mary,—The last April that father lived, lived I mean below, there were several snow-storms, and the birds were so frightened and cold, they sat by the kitchen door. Father went to the barn in his slippers and came back with a breakfast of grain for each, and hid himself while he scattered it, lest it embarrass them. Ignorant of the name or fate of their benefactor, their descendants are singing this afternoon.

As I glanced at your lovely gift, his April returned. I am powerless toward your tenderness.

Thanks of other days seem abject and dim, yet antiquest altars are the fragrantest. The past has been very near this week, but not so near as the future—both of them pleading, the latter priceless.

David's grieved decision haunted me when a little girl. I hope he has found Absalom.

Immortality as a guest is sacred, but when it becomes as with you and with us, a member of the family, the tie is more vivid. . . .

If affection can reinforce, you, dear, shall not fall.

Emily

To Louise Norcross
[1880]

What is it that instructs a hand lightly created, to impel shapes to eyes at a distance, which for them have the whole area of life or of death? Yet not a pencil in the street but has this awful power, though nobody arrests it. An earnest letter is or should be life-warrant or death-warrant, for what is each instant but a gun, harmless because "unloaded," but that touched "goes off"?

Men are picking up the apples to-day, and the pretty boarders are leaving the trees, birds and ants and bees. I have heard a chipper say "dee" six times in disapprobation. How should we like to have our privileges wheeled away in a barrel? . . .

The Essex visit was lovely. Mr. L—— remained a week. Mrs. —— redecided to come with her son Elizabeth. Aunt L—— shouldered arms. I think they lie in my memory, a muffin and a bomb. Now they are all gone, and the crickets are pleased. Their bombazine reproof still falls upon the twilight, and checks the softer uproars of the departing day.

Earnest love to Fannie. This is but a fragment, but wholes are not below.

Emily

To Mrs. Edward Tuckerman
[1880]

Dear Friend,—Your sweetness intimidates.

Had it been a mastiff that guarded Eden, we should have feared him less than we do the angel.

I read your little letter. It had, like bliss, the minute length.

It were dearer had you protracted it; but the sparrow must not propound his crumb.

We shall find the cube of the rainbow,
Of that there is no doubt;
But the arc of a lover's conjecture
Eludes the finding out.

Confidingly,
Emily

To Sally Jenkins
[1880]

Atmospherically it was the most beautiful Christmas on record. The hens came to the door with Santa Claus, the pussies washed themselves in the open air without chilling their tongues, and Santa Claus—sweet old gentleman—was even gallanter than usual. Visitors from the chimney were a new dismay, but all of them brought their hands so full and behaved so sweetly, only a churl could have turned them away. And then the ones at the barn were so happy! Maggie gave the hens a check for potatoes, each of the cats had a gilt-edged bone, and the horse had new blankets from Boston.

Do you remember dark-eyed Mr. Dickinson who used to shake your hand when it was so little it had hardly a stem? He, too, had a beautiful gift of roses from a friend away. It was a lovely Christmas. But what made you remember me? Tell me with a kiss—or is it a secret?

Emily

To Louise and Fannie Norcross
[Spring, 1881]

The divine deposit came safely in the little bank. We have heard of the "deeds of the spirit," but are his acts gamboge and pink? A morning call from Gabriel is always a surprise. Were we more fresh from Eden we were expecting him—but Genesis is a "far journey." Thank you for the loveliness.

We have had two hurricanes within as many hours, one of which came near enough to untie my apron—but this moment the sun shines, Maggie's hens are warbling, and a man of anonymous wits is making a garden in the lane to set out slips of bluebird. The moon grows from the seed. . . . Vinnie's pussy slept in grass Wednesday—a Sicilian symptom—the sails are set for summer, East India wharf. Sage and saucy ones talk of an equinoctial, and are trying the chimneys, but I am "short of hearing," as the deaf say. Blessed are they that play, for theirs is the kingdom of heaven. Love like a rose from each one, and Maggie's a Burgundy one she ardently asks.

Emily

To Louise and Fannie Norcross
[1881]

The dear ones will excuse—they knew there was a cause. Emily was sick, and Vinnie's middle name restrained her loving pen.

These are my first words since I left my pillow—that will make them faithful, although so long withheld. We had another fire—it was in Phoenix Row, Monday a week ago, at two in the night. The horses were harnessed to move the office—Austin's office, I mean. After a night of terror, we went to sleep for a few moments, and I could not rise. The others bore it better. The brook from Pelham saved the town. The wind was blowing so, it carried the burning shingles as far as Tom's piazza. We are weak and grateful. The fire-bells are oftener now, almost, than the church-bells. Thoreau would wonder which did the most harm.

The little gifts came sweetly. The bulbs are in the sod—the seeds in homes of paper till the sun calls them. It is snowing now. . . . "Fine sleighing we have this summer," says Austin with a scoff. The box of dainty ones—I don't know what they were, buttons of spice for coats of honey—pleased the weary mother. Thank you each for all.

The beautiful words for which L—— asked were that genius is the ignition of affection—not intellect, as is supposed, —the exaltation of devotion, and in proportion to our capacity for that, is our experience of genius. Precisely as they were uttered I cannot give them, they were in a letter that I do not find, but the suggestion was this.

It is startling to think that the lips, which are keepers of thoughts so magical, yet at any moment are subject to the seclusion of death.

. . . I must leave you, dear, to come perhaps again . . .

Emily

To Mrs. J. G. Holland
[On the death of Dr. Holland, October, 1881]

We read the words, but know them not. We are too frightened with sorrow. If that dear, tired one must sleep, could we not see him first?

Heaven is but a little way to one who gave it, here. "Inasmuch," to him, how tenderly fulfilled!

Our hearts have flown to you before—our breaking voices follow. How can we wait to take you all in our sheltering arms?

Could there be new tenderness, it would be for you, but the heart is full—another throb would split it—nor would we dare to speak to those whom such a grief removes, but we have somewhere heard "A little child shall lead them."

Emily

317

To *Mabel Loomis Todd*
[On receipt of a painting of the flower called
Indian Pipe, 1882]

Dear Friend,—That without suspecting it you should send
me the preferred flower of life, seems almost supernatural,
and the sweet glee I felt at meeting it I could confide to none.
I still cherish the clutch with which I bore it from the ground
when a wondering child, an unearthly booty, and maturity
only enhances mystery, never decreases it. To duplicate the
vision is even more amazing, for God's unique capacity is too
surprising to surprise. I know not how to thank you. We do
not thank the rainbow, although its trophy is a snare.

To give delight is hallowed—perhaps the toil of angels,
whose avocations are concealed.

I trust you are well, and the quaint little girl with the deep
eyes, every day more fathomless.

With joy,
E. Dickinson

To *Louise and Fannie Norcross*
[November, 1882]

Dear Cousins,—I hoped to write you before, but mother's
dying almost stunned my spirit.

I have answered a few inquiries of love, but written little
intuitively. She was scarcely the aunt you knew. The great
mission of pain had been ratified—cultivated to tenderness
by persistent sorrow, so that a larger mother died than had
she died before. There was no earthly parting. She slipped
from our fingers like a flake gathered by the wind, and is now
part of the drift called "the infinite."

We don't know where she is, though so many tell us.

I believe we shall in some manner be cherished by our
Maker—that the One who gave us this remarkable earth has
the power still farther to surprise that which He has caused.
Beyond that all is silence. . . .

Mother was very beautiful when she had died. Seraphs are

solemn artists. The illumination that comes but once paused upon her features, and it seemed like hiding a picture to lay her in the grave; but the grass that received my father will suffice his guest, the one he asked at the altar to visit him all his life.

I cannot tell how Eternity seems. It sweeps around me like a sea. . . . Thank you for remembering me. Remembrance —mighty word.

"Thou gavest it to me from the foundation of the world."

Lovingly
Emily

To Mr. James D. Clark
[1882]

Dear Friend,— . . . He never spoke of himself, and encroachment I know would have slain him. . . . He was a dusk gem, born of troubled waters, astray in any crest below. Heaven might give him peace, it could not give him grandeur, for that he carried with himself to whatever scene. . . .

E. Dickinson

To James D. Clark
[Late autumn, 1882]

Dear Friend,—It pains us very much that you have been more ill. We hope you may not be suffering now. Thank you for speaking so earnestly when our mother died. We have spoken daily of writing you, but have felt unable. The great attempt to save her life had it been successful would have been fatigueless, but failing, strength forsook us.

No verse in the Bible has frightened me so much from a child as "from him that hath not, shall be taken even that he hath." Was it because its dark menace deepened our own door? You speak as if you still missed your mother. I wish we might speak with you. As we bore her dear form through the wilderness, light seemed to have stopped.

Her dying feels to me like many kinds of cold—at times electric, at times benumbing,—then a trackless waste love has never trod. . . .

The letter from the skies, which accompanied yours, was indeed a boon. A letter always seemed to me like Immortality, for is it not the mind alone, without corporeal friend?

I hope you may tell us that you are better.

Thank you for much kindness. The friend anguish reveals is the slowest forgot.

E. Dickinson

To James D. Clark
[March, 1883]

Dear Friend,—In these few weeks of ignorance of you, we trust that you are growing stronger, and drawing near that sweet physician, an approaching spring, for the ear of the heart hears bluebirds already, those enthralling signals. . . . The great confidences of life are first disclosed by their departure, and I feel that I ceaselessly ought to thank you. . . . Our household is scarcely larger than yours—Vinnie and I and two servants composing our simple realm, though my brother is with us often each day. I wish I could show you the hyacinths that embarrass us by their loveliness, though to cower before a flower is perhaps unwise, but beauty is often timidity—perhaps oftener pain.

A soft "Where is she?" is all that is left of our loved mother, and thank you for all you told us of yours. . . .

Faithfully
E. Dickinson

To Charles H. Clark
[June 16, 1883]

Dear Friend,—Thank you for the paper. I felt it almost a
bliss of sorrow that the name so long in Heaven on earth,
should be on earth in Heaven.

Do you know if either of his sons have his mysterious face
or his momentous nature?

The stars are not hereditary. I hope your brother and him-
self resumed the tie above, so dear to each below. Your bond
to your brother reminds me of mine to my sister—early, ear-
nest, indissoluble. Without her life were fear, and Paradise a
cowardice, except for her inciting voice.

Should you have any picture of your brother, I should
rejoice to see it at some convenient hour—and though we
cannot know the last, would you sometime tell me as near
the last as your grieved voice is able? . . .

Are you certain there is another life? When overwhelmed
to know, I fear that few are sure.

My sister gives her grief with mine. Had we known in
time, your brother would have borne our flowers in his mute
hand. With tears,

E. Dickinson

To Joseph K. Chickering
[1883]

Dear Friend,—I had hoped to see you, but have no grace to
talk, and my own words so chill and burn me that the tem-
perature of other minds is too new an awe.

We shun it ere it comes,
   Afraid of joy,
Then sue it to delay,
   And lest it fly

Beguile it more and more.
   May not this be,
Old suitor Heaven,
   Like our dismay at thee?

Earnestly
E. Dickinson

To Maria Whitney
[1883]

Dear Friend,—Is not an absent friend as mysterious as a bulb in the ground, and is not a bulb the most captivating floral form? Must it not have enthralled the Bible, if we may infer from its selection? "The lily of the field!"

I never pass one without being chagrined for Solomon, and so in love with "the lily" anew, that were I sure no one saw me, I might make those advances of which in after life I should repent.

The apple-blossoms were slightly disheartened, yesterday, by a snow-storm, but the birds encouraged them all that they could—and how fortunate that the little ones had come to cheer their damask brethren!

You spoke of coming "with the apple-blossoms"—which occasioned our solicitude.

The ravenousness of fondness is best disclosed by children. . . .

Is there not a sweet wolf within us that demands its food?

I can easily imagine your fondness for the little life so mysteriously committed to your care. The bird that asks our crumb has a plaintive distinction. I rejoice that it was possible for you to be with it, for I think the early spiritual influences about a child are more hallowing than we know. The angel begins in the morning in every human life. How small the furniture of bliss! How scant the heavenly fabric!

No ladder needs the bird but skies
   To situate its wings,

Nor any leader's grim baton
Arraigns it as it sings.
The implements of bliss are few—
As Jesus says of *Him*,
"Come unto me" the moiety
That wafts the cherubim.

Emily

To Maria Whitney
[1883]

Dear Friend,—You are like God. We pray to Him, and he answers "No." Then we pray to Him to rescind the "no," and He don't answer at all, yet "Seek and ye shall find" is the boon of faith.

You failed to keep your appointment with the apple-blossoms—the japonica, even, bore an apple to elicit you, but that must be a silver bell which calls the human heart.

I still hope that you live, and in lands of consciousness. It is Commencement now. Pathos is very busy.

The past is not a package one can lay away. I see my father's eyes, and those of Mr. Bowles—those isolated comets. If the future is mighty as the past, what may vista be?

With my foot in a sling from a vicious sprain, and reminded of you almost to tears by the week and its witness, I send this sombre word.

The vane defines the wind.

Where we thought you were, Austin says you are not. How strange to change one's sky, unless one's star go with it, but yours has left an astral wake.

Vinnie gives her hand.

Always with love
Emily

To Maria Whitney
[1883]

Dear Friend,—Your sweet self-reprehension makes us look within, which is so wild a place we are soon dismayed, but the seed sown in the lake bears the liquid flower, and so of all your words.

I am glad you accept rest.

Too many disdain it. I am glad you go to the Adirondacks.

To me the name is homelike, for one of my lost went every year with an Indian guide, before the woods were broken. Had you been here it would be sweet, but that, like the peach, is later. With a to-morrow in its cupboard, who would be "an hungered"?

Thank you for thinking of Dick. He is now the horse of association.

Men are picking the grass from father's meadow to lay it away for winter, and it takes them a long time. They bring three horses of their own, but Dick, ever gallant, offers to help, and bears a little machine like a top, which spins the grass away.

It seems very much like a gentleman getting his own supper—for what is his supper winter nights but tumblers of clover?

You speak of "disillusion." That is one of the few subjects on which I am an infidel. Life is so strong a vision, not one of it shall fail.

Not what the stars have done, but what they are to do, is what detains the sky.

We shall watch for the promised words from the Adirondacks, and hope the recess will all be joy. To have been made alive is so chief a thing, all else inevitably adds. Were it not riddled by partings, it were too divine.

I was never certain that mother had died, except while the students were singing. The voices came from another life. . . .

Good-night, dear. Excuse me for staying so long. I love to

come to you. To one who creates, or consoles, thought, what an obligation!

Emily

To Louise and Fannie Norcross
[1884]

Thank you, dears, for the sympathy. I hardly dare to know that I have lost another friend, but anguish finds it out.

Each that we lose takes part of us;
A crescent still abides,
Which like the moon, some turbid night,
Is summoned by the tides.

. . . I work to drive the awe away, yet awe impels the work.

I almost picked the crocuses, you told them so sincerely. Spring's first conviction is a wealth beyond its whole experience.

The sweetest way I think of you is when the day is done, and Loo sets the "sunset tree" for the little sisters. Dear Fannie has had many stormy mornings; . . . I hope they have not chilled her feet, nor dampened her heart. I am glad the little visit rested you. Rest and water are most we want.

I know each moment of Miss W—— is a gleam of boundlessness. "Miles and miles away," said Browning, "there's a girl"; but "the colored end of evening smiles" on but few so rare.

Thank you once more for being sorry. Till the first friend dies, we think ecstasy impersonal, but then discover that he was the cup from which we drank it, itself as yet unknown. Sweetest love for each, and a kiss besides for Miss W——'s cheek, should you again meet her.

Emily

To Maria Whitney
[1884]

Dear Friend,—Has the journey ceased, or is it still progressing, and has Nature won you away from us, as we feared she would?

Othello is uneasy, but then Othellos always are, they hold such mighty stakes.

Austin brought me the picture of Salvini when he was last in Boston.

The brow is that of Deity—the eyes, those of the lost, but the power lies in the *throat*—pleading, sovereign, savage—the panther and the dove!

Each, how innocent!

I hope you found the mountains cordial—followed your meeting with the lakes with affecting sympathy.

Changelessness is Nature's change.

The plants went into camp last night, their tender armor insufficient for the crafty nights.

That is one of the parting acts of the year, and has an emerald pathos—and Austin hangs bouquets of corn in the piazza's ceiling, also an omen, for Austin believes.

The "golden bowl" breaks soundlessly, but it will not be whole again till another year.

Did you read Emily Brontë's marvellous verse?

"Though earth and man were gone,
And suns and universes ceased to be,
    And Thou wert left alone,
Every existence would exist in Thee."

We are pining to know of you, and Vinnie thinks to see you would be the opening of the burr . . .

Emily, with love

To Maria Whitney
[1884]

Dear Friend,—I cannot depict a friend to my mind till I know what he is doing, and three of us want to depict you. I inquire your avocation of Austin, and he says you are "engaged in a great work"! That is momentous but not defining. The thought of you in the great city has a halo of wilderness.

Console us by dispelling it. . . .

Vinnie is happy with her duties, her pussies, and her posies, for the little garden within, though tiny, is triumphant.

There are scarlet carnations, with a witching suggestion, and hyacinths covered with promises which I know they will keep.

How precious to hear you ring at the door, and Vinnie ushering you to those melodious moments of which friends are composed.

This also is fiction.

I fear we shall care very little for the technical resurrection, when to behold the one face that to us comprised it is too much for us, and I dare not think of the voraciousness of that only gaze and its only return.

Remembrance is the great tempter.

Emily

To Louise and Fannie Norcross
[July, 1884]

Dear Cousins,—I hope you heard Mr. Sanborn's lecture. My "Republican" was borrowed before I waked, to read till my own dawn, which is rather tardy, for I have been quite sick, and could claim the immortal reprimand, "Mr. Lamb, you come down very late in the morning." Eight Saturday noons ago, I was making a loaf of cake with Maggie, when I saw a great darkness coming and knew no more until late at night. I woke to find Austin and Vinnie and a strange physician bending over me, and supposed I was dying, or had died, all was so kind and hallowed. I had fainted and lain unconscious for the first time in my life. Then I grew very sick and gave the others much alarm, but am now staying. The doctor calls it "revenge of the nerves;" but who but Death had wronged them? F——'s dear note has lain unanswered for this long season, though its "Good-night, my dear," warmed me to the core. I have all to say, but little strength to say it; so we must talk by degrees. I do want to know about Loo, what pleases her most, book or tune or friend. . . .

Emily

To Mrs. Edward Tuckerman
[April, 1885]

Dear Friend,—We want you to wake—Easter has come and gone.

Morning without you is a dwindled dawn.

Quickened toward all celestial things by crows I heard this morning, accept a loving caw from a

Nameless friend
"Selah"

To an unknown recipient
[1885]

Dear Friend,—I thank you with wonder. Should you ask me my comprehension of a starlight night, awe were my only reply, and so of the mighty book. It stills, incites, infatuates, blesses and blames in one. Like human affection, we dare not touch it, yet flee, what else remains?

But excuse me—I know but little. Please tell me how it might seem to you.

How vast is the chastisement of beauty, given us by

our Maker! A word is inundation, when it comes from the sea.

Peter took the marine walk at the great risk.

E. Dickinson

To Joseph K. Chickering
[1885]

Dear Friend,—The Amherst heart is plain and whole and permanent and warm.

In childhood I never sowed a seed unless it was perennial —and that is why my garden lasts.

We dare not trust ourselves to know that you indeed have left us.

The fiction is sufficient pain. To know you better as you flee, may be our recompense.

I hope that you are well, and nothing mars your peace but its divinity—for ecstasy is peril.

With earnest recollection

E. Dickinson

To Louise and Fannie Norcross
[March, 1886]

I scarcely know where to begin, but love is always a safe place. I have twice been very sick, dears, with a little recess of convalescence, then to be more sick, and have lain in my bed since November, many years, for me, stirring as the arbutus does, a pink and russet hope; but that we will leave with our pillow. When your dear hearts are quite convenient, tell us of their contents, the fabric cared for most, not a fondness wanting.

Do you keep musk, as you used to, like Mrs. Morene of Mexico? Or cassia carnations so big they split their fringes of berry? Was your winter a tender shelter—

perhaps like Keats's bird, "and hops and hops in little journeys"?

Are you reading and well, and the W——s near and warm? When you see Mrs. French and Dan give them a tear from us.

Vinnie would have written, but could not leave my side. Maggie gives her love. Mine more sweetly still.

Emily

To Charles H. Clark
[April 15, 1886]

Thank you, dear friend, I am better. The velocity of the ill, however, is like that of the snail. I am glad of your father's tranquillity, and of your own courage. Fear makes us all martial.

I could hardly have thought it possible that the scholarly stranger to whom my father introduced me, could have mentioned my friend, almost itself a vision, or have still left a legend to relate his name. With the exception of— . . . your name alone remains.

"Going home," was he not an aborigine of the sky?

The last time he came in life I was with my lilies and heliotropes. Said my sister to me, "The gentleman with the deep voice wants to see you, Emily"—hearing him ask of the servant.

"Where did you come from?" I said, for he spoke like an apparition. "I stepped from my pulpit to the train," was his simple reply; and, when I asked, "how long?"—"twenty years," said he, with inscrutable roguery.

But the loved voice has ceased; and to some one who heard him "going home" it was sweet to speak. . . . Thank you for each circumstance, and tell me all you love to say. . . .

Excuse me for the voice, this moment immortal.

E. Dickinson

To *Louise and Fannie Norcross*
[May 14, 1886, the day before her death]

Little Cousins,—Called back.

Emily

INDEX OF FIRST LINES
OF POEMS

333

INDEX OF RECIPIENTS
OF LETTERS